FOOD NO MATTER WHAT!

FOOD NO MATTER WHAT!

stories & recipes
for perfect dining
in an imperfect
world

Laura Szabo-Cohen   Karin Kasdin

SIBYL
PUBLICATIONS

Portland, Oregon

Published by SIBYL Publications, Inc. • 1007 S.W. Westwood Drive • Portland, Oregon • 97201
(503) 293-8391 • 800-240-8566

ISBN 1-889531-02-2

Graphic Design: *Design Studio Selby*

6 5 4 3 2 1

Cataloging in Publication Data

Szabo-Cohen, Laura.
     Food no matter what! : stories & recipes for
    perfect dining in an imperfect world / Laura
    Szabo-Cohen, Karin Kasdin. -- 1st ed.
       p. cm.
       Includes index.
       ISBN: 1-889531-02-2

       1. Cookery. 2. Food--Psychological aspects.
    3. Menus. I. Kasdin, Karin. II. Title.

TX728.S92 1999   641.5'6
             QBI98-1752

Printed in Canada

Contents

For — who else? — our mothers,
Hilda Chovnick Szabo and
Phyllis Schwartz Kasdin

Contributors

(in alphabetical order)

Judee Algazi

Gail Check

Edye Kamensky

Phyllis Kasdin

Karen Kossar

K'leen Mayberry

Jacqueline Orr Miller

Hilda Szabo

Ryta Weiner

Marilyn Weinstein

Additional thanks go to several people whose contributions were of the non-food variety, and just as deeply appreciated:

AOL Homeschooling Information and Discussion Board: Point/Counterpoint Folder, Michele and Andrew Hay, Jadwiga Kloda, Barbara Labanosky, Ruth LoPresti, Michelle and Kirsten Mathas, Agata Nowak, Kathy Payne, Paule Prebus, Victoria Pressner, the Rhondas, Joann Sachs, Dr. Wendy Warner Tinsley, and Stephen A. Weiner.

Introduction

It is an ancient, visceral, honorable joy to gather the bountiful, variegated, raw ingredients of a generous Earth, transform them into a whole greater than the sum of their parts, and present them—with deep intention, efficiency, delight, and a touch of pride bordering on smugness—to yourself and the other people in your life whose bodies and emotions are central to you.

But what do you do if your nail polish is wet?

If you glance at our chapter titles, you will discover we have gone, sometimes bravely and sometimes ridiculously, where no cookbook has gone before. You will discover this book contains the answers to culinary dilemmas so pervasive—but either so hopeless, embarrassing, amorphous, overwhelming, or shallow—that you have repressed labeling them. There is only one way to label them—Actual Real Life.

How to Use This Book

If we ruled the world, we would have you read each chapter from beginning to end like the little story it is. Being benevolent monarchs, we would not care in what order you read the chapters. Each chapter sets up an Actual Real Life dilemma. Then we solve everything with recipes. But that's not all. Be sure to read the "Later" addendum following each story's recipe segment. Not only will this give you closure, it will be your favorite part of the story. Enjoy!

However, since we don't rule the world, here are your other options.

1. Read the table of contents. See what tickles your fancy or applies to your life. Cook things from those chapters.

    — OR —

2. Read the book as you would a novel, from beginning to end, or as you would a magazine, leafing through it at random. Don't cook anything. Just read.

3. We include multiple entrée options within many chapters, but that doesn't mean you should serve chicken, shrimp, and pork at a dinner party. There are several menu suggestions for each scenario we describe. Mix and match hors d'oeuvres, salads, soups, entrées, side dishes, and desserts from among the recipe options.

4. Except for baking, salt means kosher (coarse) salt. Pepper always means freshly ground black pepper. Olive oil means extra virgin.

5. We use the terms "stock" and "broth" interchangeably, along with reconstituted powdered "boullion."

1 Auto-Mat
Food for Families on the Road to Everywhere

Getting your heart's desire can't be assured by spending a small fortune.
—Advertisement from Architectural Digest

Marcel French, the da Vinci of kitchen interiors, had outdone himself on Frieda's kitchen. The granite on her countertops was custom-quarried in Bangor. Her Viking oven could turn out restaurant-quality meals for three hundred. Her backsplash matched her skintones. The work stations were situated so that multiple cooks could chat companionably while not stepping over each other on the way to the spice armoire. What a shame Frieda never had a chance to cook so much as a slice of toast.

Julia, her jock daughter, was on the travel soccer team, the intermural basketball team, and the all-star baseball team. Consequently, she was also on the Sylvan Learning Center Team. Sam, her musician son, played violin in the Middlebury Junior High School Orchestra, flute in the county-wide Honors Band, bassoon in the district wind ensemble, and bass guitar for the Matricide. Both kids went to Catholic Religious Education and regular orthodontist appointments. And there actually were times when Frieda herself had some place to go. Dinner five out of seven days a week was inhaled in the ancient wreck of a car she drove in order to keep Marcel in Armani.

That was it! Idea! Frieda would call Marcel immediately and have him work his magic on her mini-van!

What to serve?

Healthy Hoagies (Subs, Grinders, Torpedos, etc.)

Whole wheat hoagie rolls (or baguettes for the sophisticated palate)

Dijon or other mustard

Sliced turkey breast

Sliced low-fat Muenster and/or provolone cheese

Shredded lettuce

Sliced tomatoes, cucumbers, and onions

Bean sprouts

Shredded carrots

Optional: **sliced jalapeño or cherry peppers**

Slice rolls open and spread with Dijon or the mustard of your children's choice, and pile on any combination of the remaining ingredients.

Close sandwich and roll tightly in foil. Child can peel the foil back as he/she eats.

Anything that can be put onto a hoagie roll can also be rolled into a tortilla. Some children like to melt cheese onto a tortilla, roll it up, and eat it cold.

NEAT MEAT-VEGGIE BALLS

1 cup very finely minced carrots

1/2 cup minced onion

3 garlic cloves, chopped

1 pound extra lean ground beef

1 pound ground turkey

1 10-oz. package frozen chopped
   spinach, defrosted, undrained

4 tablespoons minced fresh basil or
   1 teaspoon dried basil

1/2 teaspoon dried thyme

Pepper to taste

1 cup whole wheat bread crumbs

2/3 cup V-8 juice

2 eggs or 2 egg whites

Preheat oven to 400 degrees.

Steam or sauté carrots, onions, and garlic. Add to everything else in large bowl. Yes, you have already put everything else into a large bowl. Thoroughly combine by hand. Form into large meatballs, small meatballs, meatloaf … or topiary. But really, the point is this mixture can serve any purpose you want, including that of hamburgers. For medium-sized meatballs, place on baking sheet which has been sprayed with cooking oil spray. Bake 10 minutes, turn and bake 10 minutes more. Adjust cooking times for larger or smaller formations.   *Serves 6*

SPINACH-TUNA BALLS

2 cans (3 1/2-oz.) tuna

1 1/2 cups fine bread crumbs

Dash oregano

2 packages (10-oz. each) frozen
   chopped spinach,
   cooked and drained

1/4 cup lemon juice

1 cup Parmesan cheese

Salt and pepper to taste

1 cup low-fat mayonnaise

Blend first seven ingredients. Add mayonnaise. Form into bite-sized balls. Bake on baking sheet at 350 degrees for 20 minutes. May be eaten warm or cold.   *Serves 4*

Snack Food Alternatives

Raw vegetables

Low-fat cheese cubes

Fresh fruit: The juicy stuff doesn't travel well. Stick to apples, bananas, pears, and grapes.

Less crumbly (than the ubiquitous chips) carbohydrate alternatives:

Bagel chips

Pieces of pita bread or your child's favorite bread

Graham crackers

Pretzel nuggets

A Word about Drinks

Those paper cups with lids dispensed by your local two thousand fast food chains DO NOT WORK. They are responsible for the stains that permanently decorate every mini-van in our great nation. Use your own hard plastic cups with snap-on lids or carry water in sports water bottles. If you consistently refuse to stop for soda, you'll be surprised how quickly your children will learn to drink water. One gets very thirsty in a car, especially after hoagies.

(One year) Later ...

Frieda had finally recovered financially from the cost of the new kitchen and was able to rehire her domestic help. It was time to reclaim her reputation as the Brooke Astor of Scarsdale. She instructed her staff: "Get the bookbags, sports equipment, musical instruments, my office supplies, the picnic cooler, the changes of schoolclothes and uniforms, and the dirty laundry out of the mini-van. Vacuum, dust, and disinfect it, so the exterminator can get into it. Water the philodendron on the dashboard. The house is fine, but please remove the price tags from my kitchen appliances."

2 Call Me Indigestible
When Your Partner Suffers from Acid Reflux

What is food to one man may be fierce poison to others.   —Lucretius

2:00 am   Sound of gagging coming from the master bath. Ruth turns over in bed and puts the pillow over her head. More gagging. Ruth manages to fall asleep.

3:15 am   Ruth rolls over to give her hubby a hug. She playfully grabs him where his chest should be. She hugs his knees. He is sitting upright. Asleep.

6:30 am   Harvey, dressed and ready for work, leans over the bed to kiss Ruth good-bye. As he staggers out of the bedroom, he calls to her, "Great gazpacho last night, honey!"

9:00 am   Ruth is still in bed, too depressed to move. If she moved she would have to start the day. Starting the day meant thinking about dinner. It's a sad day when dinner means thinking about disease. In Ruth's case disease meant gastro-esophageal reflux disorder—not her's, Harvey's.

The culinary challenge was aggravated by their children's pickiness. Aliza and Eva wouldn't eat anything slimy, chunky, slippery, brown, green, broiled, or fragrant.

That left red, round, and flat. Harvey could die from red, round, and flat. Ruth had to please everyone. So she stayed in bed.

About GERD

GERD is a condition in which the sphincter muscle between the stomach and the esopha-gus spasms and allows acid from your previously eaten meal to journey in the wrong direction: up. The discomfort ranges from a mild burning sensation (often called heart-burn), to a gross but bearable bile-like uprising, to chest pains so severe some sufferers fear they're having a heart attack. The dietary prescription is simple and not unlike the boring guidelines most food programs for both the sick and healthy now demand—low fat, low sugar, high fiber. In addition, GERD sufferers should avoid spicy foods, which, in more serious cases, include onions, garlic, and other reactive vegetables. Alcohol is strictly forbidden. And whatever you're eating and drinking, stop eating and drinking it at least five hours before bedtime.

The non-food counsel is: Sleep propped up on a foam wedge pillow, or raise the head of your bed several inches. The GERD game is all about gravity. Keep yourself upright so your digestive tract gets all the help it needs to do its job. While doctors often medicate for this condition, and people have self-medicated their heartburn for years, medicine doesn't alter one iota the necessity of adopting an anti-acidic diet.

What to serve?

EGGPLANT AND WALNUT SPREAD

1 large eggplant
¹/₄ cup chopped onion
1 clove garlic
1 teaspoon salt
¹/₈ teaspoon pepper
2 tablespoons lemon juice
¹/₄ cup fresh parsley, chopped
¹/₄ cup chopped walnuts
3 ripe plum tomatoes, chopped

Pierce eggplant and microwave on high for 7–9 minutes, turning over once after 4 minutes. Cool. Slice eggplant in half lengthwise and scoop out the insides. Place eggplant in bowl of food processor along with next six ingredients. Stir in chopped walnuts and tomatoes, and chill overnight. Serve on wedges of pita bread.

Serves 10 as appetizer

PUMPKIN SAFFRON RISOTTO

6 cups low-salt, low-fat chicken broth, divided

$1/2$ teaspoon saffron threads, crushed, divided

2 tablespoons butter

1 cup finely chopped onion

3 cups arborio rice

1 cup dry white wine

1 can (16-oz.) solid packed pumpkin

$1/2$ cup freshly grated Parmesan cheese

Salt and pepper

Additional Parmesan cheese

Combine $1/4$ cup broth and saffron in bowl. Bring $5\,3/4$ cups broth to boil in heavy medium saucepan over high heat. Reduce heat to low and keep warm. Melt 1 tablespoon butter in large, heavy saucepan over medium heat. Add onion and sauté until soft, about 5 minutes. Add rice and stir 2 minutes. Add wine and simmer until almost no liquid remains, stirring often, about 2 minutes. Mix in pumpkin.

Add 1 cup hot broth to rice mixture; simmer until absorbed, stirring frequently, about 3 minutes. Continue adding broth 1 cup at a time until rice is tender, but still firm to bite and mixture has a thick oatmeal consistency. Stir often and allow each addition of broth to be absorbed before adding the next, about 30 minutes total. Pour saffron broth into risotto. Add 1 tablespoon butter and $1/2$ cup Parmesan. Season with salt and pepper. Serve, passing additional Parmesan separately. *Serves 12*

LOW-FAT VEGETABLE SOUP

3 medium zucchini, sliced

2 medium carrots, sliced

10 mushrooms, sliced

1 medium onion, sliced

1 10-ounce russet potato, peeled, cut into
  1-inch pieces

3 cans (14^1/$_2$-oz. each) vegetable broth

3 cups canned crushed tomatoes with
  added purée

1 can (14^1/$_2$-oz.) stewed tomatoes

3 tablespoons chopped fresh parsley

Optional: 2 tablespoons chopped cilantro

1 tablespoon chopped garlic

1 teaspoon dried basil

1 teaspoon dried oregano

Combine zucchini, carrots, mushrooms, onion, and potato in heavy large pot. Add vegetable broth, crushed tomatoes, stewed tomatoes, parsley, cilantro, garlic, basil and oregano. Bring mixture to boil. Reduce heat, cover and simmer until vegetables are tender, about 30 minutes.

Strain cooking liquid into large saucepan; reserve vegetables. Place 3 cups vegetables in blender. Add ^{1}/$_4$ cup cooking liquid. Purée until smooth. Stir purée into remaining cooking liquid in saucepan. Return remaining vegetables to cooking liquid. Season to taste with salt and pepper. (Can be prepared five days ahead. Cover and refrigerate.)   *Serves 6–8*

GRILLED TUNA WITH WARM MANGO SALAD

1 large mango, pitted, peeled, cut into
  ^{1}/$_2$-inch cubes

^{1}/$_2$ cup fresh pineapple, cut into
  bite-sized cubes

1 tablespoon snipped scallions

1 tablespoon olive oil

Juice of two limes

Four 6-ounce tuna steaks about
  1-inch thick

Mix first four ingredients together and sauté briefly.

Prepare barbecue or preheat broiler. Squeeze lime juice over each steak and grill about 4 minutes per side or until just opaque in center. Top each steak with a generous portion of mango salad.   *Serves 4*

Rustic Baked Lemon Chicken

**One 3¹/₂-pound chicken, cut
into 10 pieces**

1 teaspoon salt

¹/₄ teaspoon pepper

Flour for dredging

2 tablespoons olive oil

1¹/₂ tablespoons thinly sliced garlic

8 fresh thyme sprigs

1¹/₂ cups chicken stock

2 lemons

Preheat oven to 400 degrees. Season chicken pieces with salt and pepper.

Dredge chicken in flour. In 10-inch oven-proof skillet heat 1 tablespoon olive oil over medium heat. Sauté chicken pieces to a rich golden brown. Transfer to a plate and reserve. Discard fat from skillet and add remaining oil. Add garlic and cook over moderate heat for 2 minutes. Remove from heat.

Spread thyme sprigs over the garlic. Arrange browned chicken pieces side by side. Add chicken stock. Cut 1 lemon into 10 slices, removing the seeds, and place 1 slice atop each piece of chicken. Squeeze the other lemon into a strainer over the chicken. Return skillet to heat and bring stock to a simmer. Cover and place in oven.

After 15 minutes, baste the chicken with cooking liquid. Continue cooking, uncovered, for an additional 35 to 40 minutes, basting every 10 minutes. When done, chicken and lemon slices will be nicely browned. Transfer to platter and serve with mashed potatoes and spinach.

Serves 6

ANGEL HAIR WITH ROASTED VEGETABLES AND MARINARA SAUCE

2 small zucchini

1 medium eggplant

2 small yellow squash

12 mushrooms

12 asparagus spears

1 large red onion (may be discarded after roasting, but use an onion for the way its flavor infuses the rest of the vegetables)

Olive oil spray

5 cloves garlic, minced

$1/4$ cup dry white wine (the alcohol dissipates when wine is cooked)

5 tablespoons chicken or vegetable broth

1 pound angel hair pasta, cooked

Bottled marinara sauce

Preheat oven to 400 degrees. Place vegetables in large baking pan. Spray them with olive oil spray until they are very thinly coated. Sprinkle minced garlic over vegetables. Add wine and broth. Roast in oven for 1 hour.

Slice roasted vegetables into bite-sized chunks. Serve over angel hair with 2 tablespoons of your favorite, low-fat marinara sauce on each portion.

Serves 4–6

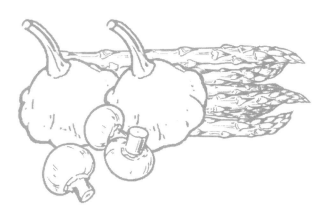

SWEET POTATO PIE

CRUST:

Vegetable oil cooking spray

2 cups graham cracker crumbs

2 teaspoons ground cinnamon

1 large egg white

FILLING:

4 medium sweet potatoes, baked

Whites from 6 large eggs

1/4 teaspoon ground nutmeg

1/4 teaspoon ground cloves

1/8 teaspoon ground allspice

1/2 teaspoon ground ginger

2 tablespoons vanilla

1 teaspoon orange peel

4 tablespoons pure maple syrup

6 ounces fat-free cream cheese

1/4 cup freshly squeezed orange juice

Preheat oven to 350 degrees. Spray 10-inch pie pan with vegetable spray to coat. Place all remaining ingredients for crust in bowl of food processor. Pulse until mixed. Transfer crust mixture to pan and press down firmly, covering the bottom.

FILLING: Peel potatoes, then place in mixing bowl and mash with a fork. Transfer potatoes to processor or blender and add all remaining filling ingredients. Process until smooth and blended. Pour filling into crust.

Bake for 30–45 minutes until center of pie is firm and not sticky. Cool on rack for 30 minutes and refrigerate for 1 hour. Serve cold.

Serves 8

Tofu Cheesecake

2 pounds firm tofu

3 tablespoons lemon juice

1 tablespoon vanilla

$^1/_2$ teaspoon salt

$^1/_4$ cup oil

$^1/_2$ cup honey

1 cup sugar

1 prebaked 10-inch graham cracker
pie shell

Fresh fruit, sliced attractively

Preheat oven to 375 degrees. Beat first seven ingredients together until smooth and creamy. Pour into crust and bake 40 minutes. Top with fresh cut fruit of your choice. *Serves 8*

Orange-Glazed Baked Bananas

1 tablespoon orange juice concentrate

1 teaspoon sugar

$^1/_2$ teaspoon vanilla

1 teaspoon rum extract

4 ripe bananas, peeled

2 cinnamon sticks, each cut in half

Preheat oven to 450 degrees. In small bowl, mix orange juice concentrate, sugar, vanilla, rum extract, and 2 tablespoons water. Place a banana and $^1/_2$ cinnamon stick on a piece of foil large enough to completely encase the banana. Spoon one quarter of orange mixture over each banana and wrap foil to form a package. Set packages on baking sheet and bake 15 minutes. Discard cinnamon. May be eaten plain or served with fat-free vanilla frozen yogurt. *Serves 4*

(Three days) Later ...

2:00 am   Z z z z z z z z z z z z z z z z z z

3:30 am   Z z z z z z z z z z z z z z z z z z

4:00 am   Ruth, after hours of trying to rouse Harvey, took a cold shower and went back to sleep.

3 Banana Splitsville
Comfort Foods during Divorce and Other Difficult Life Passages

A woman is like a teabag. Only in hot water do you realize how strong she is.
—Nancy Reagan

One less person would be sharing the events of the day at dinner tonight. Despite lessons and sports and deadlines, somehow the Kendalls had always managed to be seated around the big pine table at six o'clock.

But the big pine table didn't fit into either Janice's or Phil Kendall's new separate apartments, and no one was terribly hungry tonight. Janice, having used up all her sick and vacation days consorting with lawyers, mediators, and family therapists, had had to work today or risk losing her job. So despite it being her first day in the new apartment and her first stab at single motherhood, she was unable to shop for a new table or the stuff to put on it. Sagging in her pinstripe pantsuit at 5:45 in the 7-Eleven, she cased the freezers for something fast and cheap to please Joey and Nate. But Janice herself was frozen: There wasn't an entrée in the world which would please her sons tonight. And she didn't have an erg left over for so much as pressing a button on the microwave.

WHAT TO SERVE?

Just writing this is making us crave ice cream. Not frozen yogurt. Not Tofutti. Real, rich, comforting ice cream and we know those kids would like it too. We are not advocating substance abuse, in this case food, as a long-term coping strategy, but some situations that may call for an isolated binge may be divorce and a difficult move, job loss, severed friendships, non-injurious but scary accidents, and crushing (not merely disappointing) blows to the egos of both children and adults in the workplace, on the playing fields, in the classroom, or in any other public arena.

That night, Janice served her children banana splits on TV tables. Here are some other ideas:

Strawberry shortcake
Apple pie à la mode
Eclairs, cannoli, and other oozy baked goods
Sticky buns
Classic chocolate cake
Lemon meringue pie
Milkshakes
Cheesecake
All the soda anyone wants with any of the above

If it's fats, not sweets, that do it for you and the kids:

Pizza With The Works
You-should-excuse-the-expression McDonald's, Burger King, Wendy's, KFC, etc.
Nachos slathered with melted cheese and salsa
Foot-long hoagies (not the healthy ones we have in chapter 1. Auto-Mat)

LATER ...

Termination must have been in the air. That night was the television premiere of "Terminator 2." The only thing that could bring more joy to the boys than the banana splits was cinematic violence and carnage. Between rooting for Arnold and lapping up Redi-Whip, the boys were able to release tears and fears. Joey cried freely for the first time since the news and his family had been broken. Nate asked accusatory questions during the commercials which Janice answered patiently. After the boys had finally settled down in the first bedroom they had ever shared, Janice washed and put away the boys' bowls. She purposely smashed her own in the sink, cleaned it up, got herself a fresh bowl, and had seconds.

4 Nailing Down Dinner
Menus for the Woman Who Just Had a Manicure

I'm tired of all this nonsense about beauty being only skin-deep. That's deep enough. What do you want—an adorable pancreas? —Jean Kerr

Origi-Nails, open only one month, was hopping. Because it provided such essential services, services without which a portion of the female population would become extinct, business was excellent. Betty and Marissa were holding a conversation across their facing manicurists' tables.

"I can't believe you, Betty. It was a lovely, spontaneous gesture to invite the office over for dinner tonight. But how could you forget after ten years of every-Thursday manicure appointments that you can never cook for company on a Thursday? Your nails won't be DRY!"

"Early menopause. My mind is deoxygenated. Truthfully, Marissa, forgetting that I won't be able to work with beets, turmeric, or Brillo is nothing compared to forgetting my firstborn's name for the last two weeks."

WHAT TO SERVE?

TOUCH-ME-NOTS (THE MANICURE DON'TS)

Beets

Turmeric

Mustard Seed

Teabags

Raspberries, blueberries, etc.

Dough

Shish-kebob

Flour, cornmeal, or anything that is grainy and can stick to polish

Anything that needs to be shaped

Anything that needs to be dipped and/or breaded

Steel wool and other abrasive scrubbing devices

Abrasive cleansers

Sponges (your fingers slip in the holes)

NAIL-FRIENDLY CAVIAR APPETIZER

Spread one container of **soft cream cheese** into a shallow serving dish. Cover with **red caviar** and **chopped red onion**. Use an onion holder for chopping. This looks like a large comb. The prongs hold the onion in place while you slice. Surround with crisp crackers.

HILDA'S SPICED NUTS

1 egg white

1 teaspoon water

4 cups canned mixed nuts, or your favorite combination of pecans, walnuts, peanuts, almonds, hazelnuts, etc. Without their shells, of course.

$^3/_4$ cup sugar

$1^1/_2$ teaspoons cinnamon

$1^1/_2$ teaspoons nutmeg

$^1/_2$ teaspoon allspice

$^1/_2$ teaspoon salt (omit if using the pre-salted canned variety of mixed nuts)

Vegetable oil spray

Preheat oven to 350 degrees. Place your oven shelf in the mid-oven position. In a mixing bowl, lightly beat together egg white and water. Add nuts, and using two spoons, toss gently to coat.

Thoroughly combine sugar, spices, and salt in small bowl. Add to nuts and toss to coat. Place spiced nuts in a single layer on an oil-sprayed baking sheet.

Bake 20 to 25 minutes. WATCH IT … this likes to burn! Serve in decorative bowl as appetizer, dessert, or snack.

CUCUMBER DISCS

Slice **cucumbers**. Spread with a mixture of **cream cheese** and **horseradish**. Top with pieces of **smoked fish (salmon, bluefish, trout)** and a **sprig of fresh dill**.

ITALIAN ANTIPASTO PLATTER

Arrange pre-sliced **prosciutto, salami,** and **Fontina cheese** on a platter with purchased **roasted red and yellow peppers, artichoke hearts, olives**, and **cherry tomatoes**. Serve with your favorite **vinaigrette**.

TURKEY CHILI FOR CASUAL ENTERTAINING

This recipe is delicious and can be made by just dumping the ingredients into a pot. An electric can opener is essential as is an onion holder.

1 pound ground turkey, browned

1 large onion, chopped

2 cans (19-oz. each) black beans, drained

2 cans (16-oz. each) red kidney beans, drained

2 cans (4-oz. each) diced green chiles, drained

1 can (14^1/2-oz.) stewed tomatoes

1 large can (28-oz.) whole Italian tomatoes, with liquid

^{1}/4 cup chili powder (or less if you prefer)

2 tablespoons tomato paste

Brown turkey in large pot. Add onions and cook until limp. Add remaining ingredients and cook over medium-high heat 20 minutes. This is very thick chili. Add water or tomatoes if you prefer yours thinner.

Serve with cornbread you make from a mix and a salad your husband makes from scratch.

Serves many

ELEGANT SWEET POTATOES WITH COINTREAU AND CHERRIES

4 medium sweet potatoes*
²/₃ cup brown sugar, firmly packed
¹/₄ cup water
2 tablespoons butter
1 cup dried cherries
¹/₄ cup Cointreau

Preheat oven to 375 degrees. Wash the sweet potatoes, but do not peel. Boil in water to cover until barely soft, about 15 minutes. Drain, cool, and peel. Slice into a greased casserole.

Bring to a boil the brown sugar, water, butter, and cherries. Add the Cointreau and pour the mixture over the potatoes. Bake, uncovered, 30 minutes, basting several times with the syrup in the casserole. Serve with grilled swordfish.

Serves 6

Surprisingly, canned sweet potatoes taste as good as sweet potatoes you prepare yourself, and are far healthier for your nails. Trust us: We otherwise rarely use canned vegetables.

SIMPLE SWORDFISH

Using a fork and not your nails, squeeze **fresh lime juice** over **fresh swordfish** and grill. Ta Da!

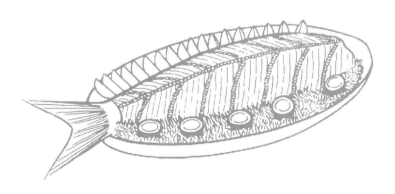

Veal Chops L'Orange

3 tablespoons olive oil

4 veal chops, 1 inch thick

Salt and pepper to taste

$1/2$ cup finely chopped Vidalia or other yellow onion

$1/3$ cup dry sherry

$1/3$ cup chicken broth

2 tablespoons orange marmalade or apricot conserve

$1/4$ cup buttermilk

Parsley for garnish

Heat oil in large skillet until very hot. Sear veal chops on both sides, seasoning with salt and pepper. Reduce heat and cook until chops are almost done, still pink in center and juicy. Remove them to a platter and cover.

Add onion to skillet and cook, covered, over medium heat until tender, about 7 minutes. Add sherry, broth, and marmalade to skillet, and boil, stirring up any pieces that stick. When mixture is reduced by one-third, whisk in buttermilk and heat one minute. Spoon sauce over chops. Garnish with parsley. *Serves 4*

Warm Winter Fruit Compote over Ice Cream or Yogurt

1 jar (12$1/2$-oz.) sour pitted cherries, drained

1 package (10-oz.) dried apricots

1 cup raisins

1 apple, cut into large chunks

1 teaspoon cinnamon

$1/2$ teaspoon nutmeg

1 cup red wine

Vanilla ice cream or frozen yogurt

Combine first six ingredients in large saucepan and stir. Add 1 cup of your favorite red wine. Port works beautifully. Heat until almost boiling. Let stand 5 minutes. Spoon over vanilla ice cream or frozen yogurt. *Makes 5 cups*

RAISIN BREAD PUDDING

12 slices cinnamon raisin bread, lightly toasted

2 tablespoons no-sugar-added apple butter

Vegetable oil spray

2 cups skim milk

1 egg

2 egg yolks

1/4 cup sugar

1/2 teaspoon vanilla

Preheat oven to 350 degrees. Using an overturned ramekin, cut toast into 12 rounds, discard trimmings. Spread 6 rounds with apple butter; cover each with another round. Spray 6 ramekins with vegetable oil spray; set a sandwich into each ramekin.

Scald milk in heavy saucepan over medium heat. Combine egg, egg yolks, sugar, and vanilla in mixing bowl. Spoon some of the hot milk into egg mixture, then stir egg mixture into remaining milk, whisking constantly until smooth. Ladle mixture into ramekins.

Arrange the ramekins in 2-inch deep baking dish. Pour enough hot water to come halfway up exteriors of ramekins, being careful not to get any water into the ramekins themselves. Bake for 40 minutes or until set. Remove from ramekins. Serve warm or chilled.   *Serves 6*

LATER ...

One week later, Betty and Marissa were talking across their facing pedicure chairs.

"Yes Marissa, it was an unqualified success. There are several little tricks, you see. One: Use recipes that involve only pouring, stirring, or shaking—Utensil Foods! Two: In a case like this, everything we learned about cooking ahead doesn't apply. You have to wait until another pair of hands arrives (a guest or your husband) who can do the final fine-motor tasks. Three: Someone else has to clean up. I'm sorry. I know that sounds self-indulgent, but it's just the way it is. So what are you doing tonight?"

"Ken and I are going to picnic on the beach. Then we're going to take a long romantic walk and feel the sand between our ... "

Note: Just in case you are not as comfortably in touch with your inner shallowness as we are, everything in this chapter also pertains to bandaged or wounded hands.

5 A Dinner Engagement
Meeting and Eating with Your Child's Betrothed

Friendships, like marriages, are dependent on avoiding the unforgivable.
—John D. MacDonald

John and Joan Piconelli were feeling old. After all, wasn't it only four days since their own wedding in 1972? And here was their firstborn, Antonia, announcing her engagement. To the boy next door. Parker.

The Piconellis had been friends with the Smythes for twenty years, ever since moving into the same cul-de-sac: The two moms had bumped into each other on their way to the other's house with a chocolate cake. For two decades Letitia and Joan traversed Gail Sheehy's "passages" together. From the Mommy-and-Me group in the fire station basement, to co-chairing Community Harvest Day, to not working out to Kathy Smith exercise videos together, Letitia and Joan did it all before "do it all" became a phrase. Their ultimate twin achievement came last year: becoming computer literate just in time to be able to e-mail their kids during their final year at the same college.

Throughout all of the above passages, the friends broke bread but not confidences. Over instant coffee, lunches out, dinners in, with and without husbands and children, the women shared secrets no one dreamed resided in their suburban hearts. Joan confessed to Letitia that Antonia's ... mood swings ... were driving her to infanticide. Letitia let on that Parker's sense of ... entitlement ... was going to prevent him from ever earning an honest dollar. Their children's union would test the fortitude of their friendship in the crucible of mutual knowledge that the other woman's kid was whacko.

In addition, there was a lesser but more immediate problem. Joan had to prepare the requisite inviting-the-future-in-laws dinner. She had to make something special for people who had eaten all her specialties three times over. One phone call from Antonia had turned Joan's best friend in the entire universe into a total stranger!

What to serve?

Hors d'Oeuvres

Life passage celebrations such as weddings and engagements merit champagne and caviar. But sometimes our budgets can't handle both. We have found no substitute for a fine champagne, but we do have two worthy substitutes for those priceless sturgeon eggs. This Tapenade, like caviar, is pungent, spreadable, and tastes of the sea. The Quinoa Caviar *feels* like those salty pearls, daintily exploding against one's palate in the self-same way … but it's cheap as mud.

TAPENADE

1 can (6-oz.) fine olive-oil packed tuna (We recommend Progresso if you can find it.) Do not drain.

1 tin of flat anchovy fillets, with oil

2 dozen dried or soft Italian or Greek olives, pitted

4 garlic cloves, peeled

2 heaping tablespoons capers

1 tablespoon Dijon mustard

2 teaspoons roasted lemon juice (see page 51) or 1 tablespoon plain fresh lemon juice is almost as wonderful.

1/4 cup cognac

Salt and pepper

Throw it all in the food processor. Process until coarsely puréed–dip consistency but not silky. Taste, then add salt and pepper to taste.

Do not succumb to the 90's urge to drain, rinse, or paper towel your anchovies and tuna free of oil. Ordinarily, tapenades demand an additional 1/4 cup of good olive oil, which we have omitted. Indeed, you may need to incorporate 2 or 3 tablespoons of water or vegetable stock to make this paste properly spreadable.

Serves 6–8

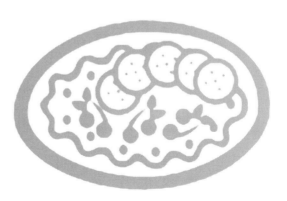

Mrs. Mayberry's Quinoa Caviar

Mrs. Mayberry says to make this the day before so it can "set up and taste like something."

1 small eggplant (10–12 ounces)

1 tablespoon extra virgin olive oil

1 onion, finely chopped

1 cup quinoa, uncooked (a grain available at health food stores and many markets)

2 cups salted water

1 shallot, minced

3 tablespoons fresh cilantro, minced

3 tablespoons parsley, chopped

5 teaspoons tamari or soy sauce

2 tablespoons lemon juice (must be fresh)

Salt and pepper to taste

Preheat oven to 350 degrees. Prick eggplant with fork and roast on oiled or nonstick baking sheet for 40 minutes or until very tender. When cool, cut in half lengthwise, and *carefully so as not to break skin*, scoop out flesh. Save the shells.

Heat oil in frying pan, and sauté onion until tender but not brown (about 4 minutes). Add quinoa to pan, stirring and toasting for about 1–2 minutes. Add salted water and bring to boil. Reduce heat, cover pan, and simmer 15 minutes. Remove from heat and let stand covered 10 minutes. Uncover, fluff the grains with a fork, and transfer to a mixing bowl. Cool thoroughly.

Put eggplant flesh, shallot, cilantro, parsley, tamari, and lemon juice in a food processor. Purée to a smooth paste. Add this eggplant paste to your mixing bowl of cooled quinoa, and stir gently but thoroughly. Add more tamari, lemon juice, and salt and pepper to taste—this dish needs a good, confident adjustment of seasonings.

Spoon mixture into reserved eggplant shells and serve exactly as you'd serve caviar: with toast points, bruschetta, on scooped out boiled potatoes, with sour cream, etc.   *Serves 8*

MARINATED GOAT CHEESE AND MUSHROOMS

A day in advance, place a **3- or 4-ounce round of goat cheese** in a small glass bowl. Slice **2–3 button mushrooms**, not too thinly. Fan them around the cheese. Cover with **Champagne Vinaigrette** (below). Refrigerate.

An hour before serving, thoroughly drain off dressing, and let cheese come to room temperature. (Even though it looks gross and murky, don't throw out that yummy mushroomy, cheesy dressing which you have drained off! Use it on a green salad the next day or on steamed new potatoes.)   *Serves 6*

CHAMPAGNE VINAIGRETTE

6 tablespoons champagne vinegar

3 tablespoons extra virgin olive oil

2 teaspoons crushed garlic

$1/4$ teaspoon dried tarragon

Put all ingredients in a glass jar and shake well.

Makes $1/2$ cup

ACCOMPANIMENTS TO HORS D'OEUVRES

One entire baguette, sliced thinly and evenly. (Your bakery or supermarket bakery can do this perfectly.) Toast slices very lightly.

Rice crackers

Thinly sliced rounds and strips of the crispest:

Cucumber

Fennel

Red bell pepper

CHARD AND CHICK-PEA SOUP

Though technically a "country" soup, this one somehow manifests as quite urbane. It can be made a day in advance and reheated.

6 cups homemade beef stock or low-salt canned beef broth

2 cups canned, drained garbanzo beans (chick-peas)

1 cup *each*, diced: white turnip, celery, yellow onion, carrot

1 cup roughly chopped Swiss chard

2 cups canned stewed tomatoes

Parmesan cheese

Combine the stock, beans, and diced vegetables in a soup pot, bring to a boil, and simmer for 30 minutes. Add chard and tomatoes; continue simmering for about 5 minutes longer. May be served with freshly grated Parmesan cheese.

Serves 6–8

DILLED CREAM OF ZUCCHINI SOUP

This recipe does not employ dill subtly. It is an aromatic and intensely herb-y first course, elegant either chilled or hot.

2 tablespoons unsalted butter

1 large onion, coarsely chopped

4 cloves garlic, sliced

8 slender zucchini, peeled and sliced

5 cups water

1 bunch dill minus a few sprigs to save for garnish*

1 cup of something white, ranging from heavy cream to whole to skim milk depending on preference and dietary demands

Salt and pepper

Melt butter in soup pot and sauté onion and garlic until transparent. Add zucchini and water, bring to boil, lower to simmer, cover, and cook until zucchini are tender, about 15 minutes. Add dill, simmer 5 minutes more. Purée mixture until smooth.

Return mixture to pot, add the cup of light cream (or whatever), season with salt and pepper to taste, heat gently for another 2–3 minutes. Do not boil. If you are serving this soup hot, it is now ready. Excellent as it is hot, we prefer it chilled, so if you wish to serve it cold, bring it to room temperature first, and then refrigerate overnight. Either way, garnish with a sprig of dill and some coarsely crushed black peppercorns.   *Serves 6–8*

*A note on fresh dill: It's sandy and gritty and the stems are not used in this dish except for garnish. So wash it three times, dry it thoroughly but gently with paper towel, pluck off the feathery leaves, and stick those yummy stems in the freezer for making stock. This degree of care is not so important when adding a tablespoon or two of chopped dill to a stew or stuffing, but this recipe is its dill, and without three rinsings it tastes like … see chapter 6. Beach Melba.

ROASTED HENS IN VERMOUTH

6 Rock Cornish game hens, large squabs, or teeny chickens (which are actually what many butchers are panning off as game hens these days)

^{1}/$_2$ teaspoon salt per bird

^{1}/$_2$ teaspoon freshly ground green peppercorns per bird

2 teaspoons grape-seed oil per bird

3 apples

3 stalks celery

3 medium onions

1 cup hot chicken stock, bouillon, or canned low-salt chicken broth

1 cup good vermouth (Sweet or dry— it doesn't matter. Each has its own superb taste.)

2–3 tablespoons melted butter or margarine

Preheat oven to 400 degrees. Season birds, inside and out, with ^{1}/$_2$ teaspoon salt and ^{1}/$_2$ teaspoon pepper *each*. (Decrease the salt if dietary regimes demand it, but not the pepper.) Rub the exterior with grape-seed oil.

Cut the apples, celery, and onions into large chunks and loosely pack into cavities.* Place hens in shallow roasting pan, breast side down, and roast 15 minutes.

Reduce heat to 325 degrees. For basting mixture, combine stock, vermouth, and butter or margarine. Roast 1 hour, or until browned and tender, basting about 4 times. Turn birds halfway through.   *Serves 6–8*

Some cooks remove this kind of "stuffing" (really just aromatics for scenting the poultry) before serving, some don't. Some guests eat it, some don't. We remove it for high occasions like this chapter's (especially since we're including a more sophisticated celery side dish), and when everyone goes home (heh-heh), we simmer it in stock to cover until it's relaxed, purée the whole thing, and taste for seasonings. This makes healthy, low-fat gravy you could shove in the freezer, then serve later over grilled chicken breasts.

GREEK HERB-ROASTED LEG OF LAMB

One 5–7 pound leg of lamb, at room temperature

6 cloves peeled garlic

2 tablespoons olive oil

1 tablespoon salt

1 teaspoon cracked black pepper

1 tablespoon fresh thyme

1 tablespoon fresh mint, chopped

1 tablespoon dried oregano

Juice of 2 lemons

3 cups boiling water

Preheat oven to 425 degrees. Rinse meat, pat it dry, and place in shallow roasting pan. Make 6 evenly spaced incisions on the fat side of the leg and insert garlic cloves. Rub entire leg with oil, salt, pepper, thyme, mint, and oregano. Roast for 30 minutes.

Reduce heat to 325 degrees. Add lemon juice and water and cook for 40 minutes to 1 hour and 15 minutes for rare lamb, or 1 hour and 30 minutes for medium. Baste frequently. (If you prefer to use a meat thermometer, insert in thickest part of leg without hitting bone, and let internal temperature reach 140 degrees for rare, 145–150 degrees for medium.)

Once removed from oven, leg of lamb needs to sit *at least* 20 minutes before being succulently, thinly, sliced. This dish needs no sauce, but if you wish to serve the pan juices, skim fat carefully.

Serves 8

Whichever of the following vegetables you choose to accompany the main dish you've selected (they all go with one another), serve the vegetable/s partially bedded on the Sweet Rice.

GREEN BEANS FANYA

1 teaspoon peanut oil

1 large bag frozen whole green beans

$^1/_4$ cup water

2 garlic cloves, sliced

Salt and pepper to taste

1 teaspoon *dark roasted* sesame oil (organic if possible)

In nonstick skillet, heat peanut oil until almost smoking. Add green beans, being careful of possible spattering. Sauté 2–5 minutes, or until they are defrosted but still uncooked. Add water and garlic, stir, then cover and let beans steam. When quite tender (this is not a dish prepared as *al dente* as we usually serve our vegetables, but it isn't mushy, either), uncover, season with salt and pepper mixing thoroughly, and turn off the heat. Drizzle with sesame oil, toss gently once more, and serve.   *Serves 6*

BRAISED HEARTS OF CELERY

2 bunches celery

4 tablespoons unsalted butter, divided in half

3 tablespoons finely chopped onion

Salt and pepper

1 cup strong beef stock—may use canned beef consommé with an extra bouillon cube added, but be careful of saltiness

¼ cup additional stock or white wine, if needed

Trim celery without mercy, only using the prime 4-inch portion of each stalk. Cut these 4-inch pieces in half. Melt 2 tablespoons butter in oven-proof sauté pan and cook onion for 4 minutes. Lay celery on top of sautéed onion; add salt, pepper, and beef stock. Cover and simmer for about 10–15 minutes or until slightly tender.

Pre-heat oven to 350 degrees. Add remaining butter to pan (and stock or wine if liquid is not covering the bottom of pan). Place pan, uncovered, in oven for 20 minutes, or until celery has absorbed all the liquid and butter. *Serves 8*

SWEET RICE

1 finely minced carrot

2 tablespoons olive oil

1 cup long grain rice

1 teaspoon salt

1 teaspoon ground cinnamon

2 teaspoons dried marjoram

3 teaspoons ground cumin

½ cup pine nuts

½ cup diced oven-dried tomatoes (see page 171)

1½ cups water

In large saucepan, sauté carrot in oil until tender. Add rice, salt, cinnamon, marjoram, cumin, and pine nuts, and sauté, stirring. Add tomatoes and stir until combined.

Add water, raise heat, and bring to boil. Cover, and turn heat to very low. Steam rice for 20 minutes without peeking. Turn off burner, don't touch that cover, and let rice sit for additional 10 minutes. Uncover, fluff with fork, and serve.   *Serves 6*

Judee's Mediterranean Stuffed Peppers

But what if your future son-in-law and his family were vegetarians? You would have to run to Judee for an entrée, just like we did. Then Judee, the best vegetarian cook in the galaxy, would give you the following recipe. The almonds, raisins, and wild rice, simmered in a lemony tomato sauce, create a savory stuffing for peppers, or any other stuff-able vegetable of your choice.

PEPPERS AND FILLING:

2 cups diced onion

4 cloves garlic, minced

2 tablespoons olive oil (or more, as Judee says, "if you dare and don't care")

^{1}/4 cup dark raisins

1 large can (28-oz.) tomatoes, chopped or, in season, 3 cups chopped fresh tomatoes

Juice of 1 whole lemon

1 teaspoon dried thyme

^{1}/2 cup tomato juice, divided

2 cups cooked "wild-and-brown rice blend" (available in health food stores and some supermarkets) or combine your own

8 ounces slivered almonds

8–10 red or green peppers (or a combination)

SAUCE:

6 tablespoons tomato paste

Juice of ^{1}/2 lemon

2 cups tomato juice

1 tablespoon sugar

^{1}/4 cup raisins

Sauté onions and garlic in oil. Add raisins, tomatoes, lemon juice, and thyme. Cook uncovered, stirring as needed. Add ^{1}/4 cup tomato juice and continue to stir. Add cooked "rice blend" and remaining ^{1}/4 cup tomato juice. Cook until all liquid is absorbed. Stir in almonds. Prepare peppers by slicing off tops and cleaning out insides. Set aside.

Combine all sauce ingredients.

ASSEMBLY: Stuff each pepper with filling and cover with its own top. Arrange peppers close together in a Dutch oven to be cooked on top of stove. Pour sauce over peppers, cover pan, and cook over medium heat for 10 minutes. Reduce heat to low, remove cover, and continue to cook, basting the peppers with the sauce, until the peppers are tender.   *Serves 8*

ENGAGEMENT CRÊPES WITH GINGERED PEAR-FIG CONSERVE

Foodie rumor has it crêpes are staging a comeback. Joan and Letitia enjoyed them the first time around smothered in Crème Anglaise. We recommend this still-rich but fashionably tailored version. The whole dish can be made and assembled one day ahead. Or, the components can be made two weeks ahead, frozen, then defrosted and assembled on the morning of your dinner.

CRÊPES:

1^{1}/2 cups sifted all-purpose flour

2 eggs

^{1}/2 cup sugar

1 teaspoon vanilla

^{1}/4 teaspoon salt

2^{1}/2 cups 2 percent or whole milk

3 tablespoons butter, melted

GINGERED PEAR-FIG CONSERVE:

10 ripe fresh figs

8 ripe pears (but not dead-ripe; you need some firmness here)

Cold water with lemon juice

^{3}/4 cup sugar

^{1}/4 cup water

1 teaspoon vanilla

^{1}/3 cup crystallized ginger, finely chopped

TOPPING:

Confectioners' sugar

Whipped cream

Toasted walnuts

In mixing bowl, combine all crêpes ingredients except milk and butter. Add milk slowly, whisking constantly. Stir in butter.

Heat a nonstick (or seasoned) 7-inch crêpe or egg pan greased lightly with butter. Pour in just enough batter so that, swirling the pan, it coats the bottom. *Lightly* brown one side (lift an edge gently to check), then flip crêpe to cook other side, but not until darkened at all; the second side of crêpes remains pale. Continue with rest of batter.

CONSERVE: Cut figs into thick dice. Peel, core, and slice pears thinly. Immerse pears in cold water with some lemon juice added to keep pears from turning color. In a skillet over medium-high heat, combine sugar and water, stirring and cooking until you achieve a caramel-colored syrup. (Be careful: At this point syrup not only likes to burn, it likes to burn the cook.) Add pears, figs, vanilla, and ginger. Simmer 20 minutes, until mixture is slightly thickened and fruit is tender but not mushy.

continued on next page

CRÊPE ASSEMBLY:

Preheat oven to 400 degrees. Place crêpe browned side up. Stripe the center with a heaping tablespoon of filling, and roll tightly and chic-ly. Place crêpes in buttered 13 x 9 x 2-inch Pyrex pan. When ready to serve, heat in oven for 10 minutes. They look pretty draped over each other on dessert plates with confectioners' sugar on top and a generous dollop of whipped cream and toasted walnuts on the side.

This recipe makes about 20 perfect crêpes (we've allowed for the tattered ones you're snacking on). So for a party of six, each guest gets three crêpes.   *Serves 6*

LOVERS' TRUFFLES

Engagement dinners, showers, weddings, Valentine's Day, anniversaries: These professional-looking candies are an idiot's delight, with no tempering or candy thermometer to mar the occasion. You may have to search a bit for the confectionery coatings, available at baker's suppliers and gourmet shops and catalogues. The rest of the ingredients are supermarket basics that end up mocha-rich, dark, and glossy.

2 packages (12-oz. each) semisweet chocolate chips

1 package (8-oz.) cream cheese, softened

3 tablespoons instant coffee granules

2 teaspoons coffee or chocolate liqueur *or* water

1 pound dark chocolate confectionery coating

Approximately 4 ounces white confectionery coating, or just enough to drizzle

In microwave or double boiler, melt the chocolate chips. Combine thoroughly with cream cheese, coffee granules, and liqueur or water. Chill until firm (about 2 hours). Roll into 1-inch balls, place on cookie sheets lined with waxed paper, and re-chill another hour or two.

In microwave or double boiler, melt the dark chocolate confectionery coating. Dip balls and replace on the lined cookie sheets to harden. Melt the white confectionery coating and, from the tip of your smallest spoon, drizzle half the truffles with the bride-to-be's initials and half with the groom's (or yours and your significant other's). This takes some dexterity, and even so the initials are wobbly, but this is okay because it has that … impromptu élan. Try a few. If you find your talents don't lie in that direction, a free-form "confectioner's squiggle" is just as elegant. Or simply skip the white coating, and nestle them on a platter or pedestal dish lined with (unsprayed) blossoms. Pure romance.

Makes about 60–65 one-inch truffles, so freeze some for the future *before* dipping in chocolate coating. You can keep them frozen for up to 3 months, then defrost in refrigerator and proceed with dipping and drizzling. *Makes 60–65 truffles*

LATER ...

From the first champagne toast to the final cognac toast, Joan cultivated a migraine figuring out how she and John could arrange their middle class lives to financially carry Antonia and her beloved-but-useless appendage Parker. Letitia bloomed hives at the nagging fear that Sylvia Plath was marrying in.

But despite the two frantically fearful mother lions whose ravaged souls continued to evaporate into the cul-de-sac ozone, dinner was a tour de force. What a luscious way to end a friendship!

6 Beach Melba
Sand-Friendly Recipes

Oh I'm goin' Surf City where it's two-to-one ...   —The Beach Boys

Jack and Dave, famous for their parties, won the Idaho State Lottery, and moved (ran, actually) from Boise to Malibu. Now they could move their galas from indoors to out, sparing them Merlot stains on the sofas and giving them a whole new aesthetic to explore—that of casual, al fresco chic. Plus, they could show off their hard-earned pecs in their Speedos. However, their signature dishes would no longer do.

The cream cheese nestling on their Caviar Rounds would sour in the sun. The mayonnaise in their Inland Potato Salad would breed the Andromeda Strain. Lobster Tails Fra Diavolo was a "mess-making" food and required special utensils. Their Silken Endive Purée would highlight every grain of sand. Their Baklava would sing a siren song to green flies.

But Jack and Dave had worshipped too often at the Shrine of Emeril to make a brutal switch to the traditional picnic-y fried drumsticks and brownies. The guys just needed ... a culinary facelift! And fast. They were hosting their first "Welcome To Us" party the next day. No time for brand new recipes based on exhaustive research. They needed a new social life NOW.

WHAT TO SERVE?

Jack and Dave's Idaho Goes Gidget Menu for 10–12 New Friends

With Some Notes on Al Fresco Packing and Serving

Jack and Dave were Tupperphobes, swell in Iowa … or Idaho or wherever we said they came from … where they served indoors and the fridge and oven were five steps away from the Ginori tureens and dining table. Malibu taught them a healthy respect for all things plastic and airtight and sandtight and burpable. Plastic storage containers stack well between freezer-paks, keeping food unsullied.

Picnic Taramosalata

1 cup olive oil (yes, really)

Juice of 2 lemons

$1/2$ pound red bliss potatoes, boiled, drained, and peeled

4 ounces carp roe (tarama or "red caviar")

$1/3$ cup finely chopped red onion

$1/3$ cup finely chopped Italian (flat-leaf) parsley

Whisk together olive oil and lemon juice. While potatoes are still piping hot, mash with carp roe. You can do this by hand or with an electric mixer, but not with your processor which will turn the mixture into bubble-gum. Beat in oil-lemon juice mixture until potatoes are fluffy. With spatula, fold in onion and parsley.

Refrigerate for 2 or more hours or up to 1 day ahead. (When not picnicking, this form of Taramosalata can actually be made 3 days ahead, but for food that will be waiting outside, it pays to be conservative on the freshness front.) Let your guests dip crackers or fill celery sticks.

Makes 1 pint

SQUASH SEEDS

Preheat oven to 325 degrees. Remove **seeds** from a **raw butternut** or **Hubbard squash**. (Hang on to that squash—we'll get there in a few minutes, see page 50.) Wipe seeds clean and dry of squash fibers. Spread them on a lightly **oiled** baking sheet and sprinkle very lightly with **salt**. Bake for 30 minutes, watching carefully for burning. Package and serve these any way you please—a sandstorm wouldn't make a difference.

BABY HAM AND CHEESE SANDWICHES

Using cocktail-size **pumpernickel or rye bread** (or a combo for bi-colored sandwiches), make sandwiches with thin slices of **Westphalian ham, Swiss** or **Jarlsburg cheese, sliced green pimiento-stuffed olives,** and **beer-mustard**. Spread mustard on the "inner" side of the cheese or ham, not on the bread itself. When each one is wrapped snugly in its own small square of foil, the sun is actually good for these Babies; it makes the cheese taste "melty" without spoiling! Pile all the silvery bundles in a bright bowl.

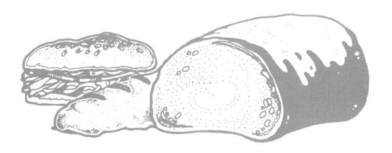

PICKLED SHRIMP

Marinate shrimp in a Pyrex pan covered with plastic wrap, then drain and transfer to plastic storage containers, in which case only toothpicks are needed.

1 cup any good quality oil you prefer

^{2}/3 cup rice wine vinegar

1 teaspoon salt

2 teaspoons celery seed

3 tablespoons undrained capers

2 pounds cleaned, cooked shrimp (about 4 dozen)

^{1}/2 bunch dill, stems and all, carefully washed and dried

1 medium onion, sliced thin

3 bay leaves

Combine first five ingredients and mix well. Place shrimp in glass or other non-reactive dish and cover with half of marinade mixture. Top with evenly-spaced dill sprigs, onion slices, and bay leaves. Pour over second half of marinade. Cover and marinate at least 24 hours. Can be made up to 3 days ahead. When ready to transport and/or serve, remove onion slices, bay leaves, dill, and drain.

Serves 10–12 for buffet or picnic

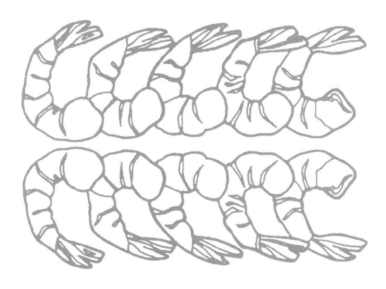

MEAT LOAF

Talk about understatement. More like a sturdy, beach-surviving paté, this rich meat loaf can be simply served in slices, or if you've omitted the Baby Ham and Cheese Sandwiches, made into immortal comfort food sandwiches on great brioche or whole wheat bread with sliced summer tomatoes.

2 pounds ground beef

¹/4 pound raw chicken livers

2 eggs

1¹/2 cups tomato juice or vegetable juice cocktail

2 cups dry bread crumbs (*must* be made from fresh bread, then left to stale overnight)

¹/3 cup coarsely chopped onion

¹/3 cup coarsely chopped green pepper

¹/2 teaspoon *each*: dry mustard, dried sage, and pepper

Preheat oven to 350 degrees. Put everything except the ground beef into food processor. Pulverize it all, especially those livers. Mix this repulsive mixture with the ground beef and pack hard into a 9 x 5 x 3-inch loaf pan. Bake 1 hour and 10 minutes, and keep checking at 10 minute intervals for firmness and doneness. Most folks like their meat loaf like they like their burgers: anywhere from medium-rare to well-done.

Cool. Drain *half* of the fat. Cover with waxed paper, and weight. The easiest way to do this is to put an identical loaf pan on top with a brick inside it.* (Velcro ankle or wrist weights work great too. Oh brave new world!) Refrigerate overnight. Serve cool or at room temperature, or hot for dinner.

Serves 10–12 for buffet or picnic

*If you're uncomfortable with this step, omit it; it will still be tasty. But it won't have that silky density, nor slice like a terrine from the Perigord even though it's just dumb old meat loaf, nor make perfect squares to fit sandwich bread, nor fan out on oval platters lined with arugula and …

SQUASH, PEAS, AND POTATOES

3 to 4 cups worth of that squash you seeded—now peeled, cut into large dices, and steamed until tender

3 cups steamed, cubed yellow or "Yukon gold" potatoes (peeling optional)

1 cup frozen peas, blanched briefly and drained

6 shallots, sliced

2 tablespoons canola oil

3 tablespoons walnut oil

Salt and pepper to taste

Place squash, potatoes, and peas in large bowl. Sauté shallots in canola oil until softened, and add to bowl along with walnut oil, salt, and pepper. Serve warm, at room temperature, or slightly chilled.

Serves 10–12 for buffet or picnic

SALADS UNDER THE SUN

The following salads purposely forego mayonnaise, making them safer hot weather fare.

WILTED SLAW WITH APPLES

**1 pound shredded green cabbage
(about 5 cups)**

**1 pound shredded red cabbage
(about 5 cups)**

1 teaspoon salt

Boiling water to cover

2 cups diced, unpeeled apples

$^1/_2$ cup finely chopped onion

$^1/_4$ cup canola or corn oil

**$^1/_3$ cup juice from roasted lemons
(recipe below) or fresh lemon juice**

3 tablespoons sugar

Pepper to taste

Put shredded cabbage into large mixing bowl and sprinkle with salt. Add boiling water to cover and let stand 10 minutes. Drain absolutely thoroughly. Add apples and onion. Whisk together oil, lemon juice, sugar, and pepper. Pour over salad and mix gently. Best made the morning of the day you serve it.

Serves 10–12

ROASTED LEMON JUICE

Like Oven-Dried Tomatoes, this is one of our recipe staples: an intensified version of its beautiful, regular fresh self. Now and again use instead of fresh lemon juice in dressings, in vegetable and grain casseroles, and sparingly on fish.

6–10 whole lemons

$^1/_3$ cup salt

Preheat oven to 375 degrees. Rub lemons with salt. Place in single layer in small casserole dish or roaster. Cover with lid or foil. Roast 1$^1/_2$ hours. Cool, halve, and juice. Pour juice into glass jar or other non-reactive container, and refrigerate. Keeps 4 days.

Makes approximately 1 cup per 8 lemons

TOMATO-KIRBY SALAD

Fitting as is for this particular menu, you also have options with this salad. Combined with ziti or macaroni it makes a fine basic pasta salad to which you may or may not add tuna, grilled chicken, etc. And when under the chandelier and not the sun, it's lovely tossed with romaine, red-leaf lettuce, and gorgonzola.

12 hefty plum tomatoes, or 3 beefsteak or slicing tomatoes (and don't even bother with this recipe if it's not tomato season), cut into mouth-manageable pieces

2 Kirby* cucumbers, sliced

1^1/$_2$ cups thinly sliced red onion

1 cup Kalamata olives, pitted and halved

^{1}/$_2$ cup olive oil

^{1}/$_4$ cup balsamic vinegar

Salt and pepper to taste

Toss everything together. Don't season to taste with salt and pepper until ready to serve— waiting in the sunshine causes salted raw vegetables to die ugly deaths.   *Serves 10–12*

*Kirby are the small cucumbers usually used for pickling. They need neither peeling nor seeding, tend to stay crisper than the more common cuke, and don't release as much water into your salad. But if you can't find Kirbys, use 1 regular cucumber, peeled, halved lengthwise, and seeded before slicing.

HOAGIE SPREAD CORNBREAD

2 cups yellow cornmeal

1 cup sifted flour

6 tablespoons sugar

$^1/_2$ teaspoon salt

$^1/_2$ teaspoon baking soda

1 tablespoon baking powder

1 stick unsalted butter, chilled and sliced into pats

3 eggs

1$^1/_2$ cups buttermilk

1 to 2 tablespoons "Hoagie Spread"— or any jarred (not canned) chopped red and green hot cherry peppers

Preheat oven to 400 degrees. Grease a 9 x 9 x 2-inch square baking pan. Process first six ingredients until just combined. Add all butter pieces at once and, pulse until mixture looks like coarse meal—do not turn this into dough.

In separate bowl, whisk together eggs, buttermilk, and hoagie spread. Add cornmeal mixture to bowl, stir well, and pour into pan. Bake 30 minutes on middle rack, until lightly brown and center set. Cut into 12 squares.

Makes 12

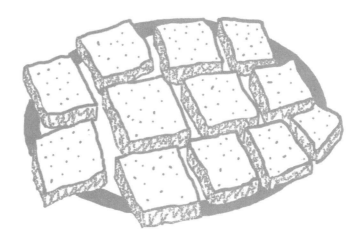

LIGHTER-THAN-AIR POPPY SEED CAKE WITH LEMON BUTTERCREAM

"Lighter" in the title implies that this is not your usual dense poppy seed loaf. It does not refer to the calorie or fat profile, which frankly, could stretch the guys' Speedos. Iced whole cakes are not the easiest thing to serve at the beach, but we've included the recipe because anything with poppy seeds is dune-friendly. (Chill cake well, pre-slice, and wrap individual slices in plastic wrap. Keep in cooler until ready to serve.) Also, by this time, Jack and Dave had purchased the Large Cake Carrier With Extra-Large Dome And Removable Handle. Bitten by the Tupperbug: Is no one immune?

CAKE:
- **2^1/2 cups flour**
- **1 cup sugar**
- **1 tablespoon baking powder**
- **^{1}/2 teaspoon salt**
- **^{1}/2 cup Wesson or vegetable oil**
- **^{3}/4 cup water**
- **5 egg yolks**
- **1 teaspoon lemon extract**
- **1 teaspoon lemon zest, grated**
- **1 can (12^1/2-oz.) poppy seed filling**
- **7 egg whites**
- **^{1}/2 teaspoon cream of tartar**

FROSTING:
- **4 cups confectioners' sugar**
- **6 tablespoons unsalted butter**
- **3–5 tablespoons whole milk**
- **1 tablespoon lemon juice**
- **1 teaspoon lemon extract**

Preheat oven to 350 degrees. In mixing bowl, combine flour, sugar, baking powder, and salt. Beat in oil, water, yolks, lemon extract, lemon zest, and poppy seed filling. The mixture should be very smooth. In clean bowl, beat egg whites and cream of tartar until stiff (but still glossy) peaks form. Fold into batter and pour mixture into an ungreased 10-inch tube pan.

Bake for 55–60 minutes, or just until cake springs back when gently poked. Invert tube pan (inverting it onto the neck of a bottle will work), and cool completely. Remove and frost.

FROSTING: Cream sugar and butter. Add milk, lemon juice, and extract. Beat until smooth and fluffy.

Optional: garnish with mint leaves and twists of lemon peel, and sprinkle with poppy seeds.

HILDA'S JAM ROLL

The crumbly, mouth-watering, Old World, real McCoy from at least three generations past. The downside of such authentic delicacies is that some measurements are descriptive instead of numeric. Worth the "vagueness," which never seems to prevent it from turning out perfectly.

DOUGH:

³/4 cup Crisco or other solid shortening

1 cup sugar

3 eggs, beaten

¹/2 cup orange juice

1 teaspoon salt

1 teaspoon vanilla

2 teaspoons baking powder

3 ¹/2–4 cups flour (or enough to give dough a workable consistency without making it heavy)

FILLING:

1 ¹/2 cups very finely chopped nuts (walnuts are the classic best, but you may substitute your favorite)

1 teaspoon maple flavoring or maple syrup

1 rounded tablespoon brown sugar

Cinnamon to taste

Grape or Strawberry Jam (quantity explained in Assembly instructions)

DOUGH: Combine all dough ingredients thoroughly. Form into ball, wrap in waxed paper and refrigerate at least 2 hours. When ready to fill and roll, divide dough into thirds, working with one third at a time, and keeping the rest refrigerated. Preheat oven to 350 degrees.

FILLING: Stir together well all ingredients except jam.

ASSEMBLY: *Hilda:* "Roll out each piece to about 7 x 11 inches, not too thin, a little thicker than a pie crust, maybe ¹/5 inch? Anyway, thin enough to be delicate but not thin enough to break and spill its guts." (She means the filling.)

"Shmear the jam on top, but not all the way to the edges. What do you mean 'How much jam?' A shmear! … somewhere between a film and a spread. Don't go overboard or the jam oozes out and crystallizes, which, now that I'm thinking, isn't the worst tragedy that can happen to a person."

Sprinkle ¹/3 nut filling on top of jam, roll up, and place on greased cookie sheet. Repeat with remaining dough and filling. Bake 30–40 minutes, or until lightly browned. Cut into ³/4- to 1-inch slices. Freezes beautifully wrapped securely in foil. Defrost and warm gently in low oven.

Makes about 30–35 slices

LATER ...

Richard Gere showed up. It was the first time anyone saw Goldie Hawn chewing. Jack and Dave and Clint are on a first-name basis. In fact, in homage to his new friends' outdoor serving savvy, Clint has cast them in cameo roles as wagon train cooks on location in Boise.

ܒ 7 Breaking Hearts and Breaking Bread
Funeral Food

The well-being of the soul can be obtained only after that of the body has been secured.   —Maimonides

Yesterday in Iowa, a twelve-year-old girl became a motherless child because of an unexpected aneurysm. In Chicago, a man's best friend couldn't spend one more day watching his parents watch him die from AIDS, and so took his own life. Right near you, a grandmother, after a long and loving ninety-six years, passed away gently, embraced by her two children and seven grandchildren. And in our own front yard, on a beautiful day in May, a beloved nineteen-year-old child/woman left this world without being able to tell her parents and brother good-bye: A suddenly out-of-control asthma attack stole her speech, breath, and life.

And even her family had to eat.

WHAT TO SERVE?

This chapter astonished us by turning out to be our most extensive, until we realized why we had been so exhaustive and deliberate with commentary and recipes. One, we had never seen the topic comprehensively addressed. And two, at no other time is food so important—except during illness, on which other food and health professionals *have* written.

This is also our only chapter where what to serve is far less important than how, when, and why to serve. While we may automatically think that loss of loved ones means loss of appetite, that is neither universally true nor permanent. And when it is true for an extended period, we must assume the age-old mantle of those who care for the bereaved—getting them to eat. Food is life.

But feeding the grieving is a sensitive process with some big goals. To provide effortless sustenance. To pack as much nourishment into as little material as possible—studies show that grieving stresses immune systems and increases nutritional needs. To give new meaning to the phrase "comfort food."

1. Cook in, or deliver in, disposable pans. Whatever you deliver food in, don't request the container be returned. Use cheap, recycled grocery containers, not the Tupperware you threw a party to get. Or use the Tupperware and make it part of your donation. Foil and plastic wrap are great as always.

    Death is not the time to be eco-green. Imagine, if you will, a household concerned with caskets, eulogies, funeral arrangements, wakes, shivas, viewings, memorials, and armies of people bringing sympathy, flowers, cards, charitable donations—and food in unlabeled containers they want returned. Get real!

2. When disposable just won't do, put a sturdy piece of tape on the bottom of the dish or utensil with your name and phone number written in permanent marker. Or, as we said above, make an outright gift of the kitchenware. Or, as we have seen lovingly done, tell the household to simply "pass the piece on," when they have to be the givers.

3. Privacy. If you are bringing food before or after the formal scheduled gatherings—food meant only for the family either immediately or for their freezer—don't make a present of your presence. Drop it off and vamoose.

4. Clean-up is a bummer even when one is not grieving. Include paper plates, cups, and napkins, and plastic utensils.

5. Attempt to contact, or be, a person who will coordinate food contributions. No one needs fifteen tuna-noodle casseroles or twenty-nine rotting fruit baskets.

6. Know your mourners' tastes, nutritional needs, and family profile. Sometimes this is tough (your boss's sister passes away), but do make an effort. Bringing chicken to vegetarians or pork roast to the kosher is not comforting.

7. Clean up. Even if there is a person employed for that purpose, be the last one to leave. During and after these occasions, there is refuse to be cleared, coffee pots to be refilled, leftovers to be packaged, labeled, refrigerated, or frozen, and garbage to be taken out. There are things to be put back in the household's cabinets, and rugs to be vacuumed. Even something as mundane as tightening the caps on soda bottles is quietly helpful.

FAMILY MENU CHOICES

We don't include any hors d'oeuvres here. After unfortunately wide experience, we've concluded that this is not the time families eat the more trivial or formal courses. Glance at the weather, then concentrate on warming soups or refreshing salads as first courses. Nor is it the time to introduce people to food with which they're completely unfamiliar; God willing, there will be other days to stretch their palates. Don't be uncreative, but concentrate on favorites. And there is absolutely no more important time for homemade bread, the staff of we-all-know-what. Strangely enough, despite our aforementioned nutrition sermon, we include more than our usual number of dessert choices. Early every Sunday morning for much of the year one of us lost a parent, our friend Stephen appeared at our door with Danish or slices of strudel. He'd hand them to us with a hug and say, "Something should be sweet."

HANNAH'S MOTHER'S SPINACH SALAD

2 teaspoons apple cider vinegar

2 tablespoons olive oil

Salt and pepper to taste

1 pound (4 cups) chopped flat-leaf
   spinach

1 Granny Smith apple, thinly sliced

4 ounces ($^1/_3$ cup) dried sour cherries

$^1/_4$ cup walnuts, very coarsely chopped

3 scallions, thinly sliced

$^1/_2$ cup seedless red grapes, halved

$^1/_3$ cup goat cheese, crumbled

Whisk together vinegar, oil, and salt and pepper. Put remaining ingredients in large bowl and toss with dressing. Serve. When sending to another household, put the salad in a plastic bag and the dressing in a small recycled glass jar.

Serves 4

CHEDDAR BROCCOLI POTATO SALAD

1 cup very coarsely chopped broccoli

2 pounds red or new potatoes, peeled
   and cubed (about 8 cups)

$^1/_2$ cup grated sharp Cheddar cheese

$^2/_3$ cup Ricotta cheese

4 cloves garlic, minced

$^1/_2$ cup chopped red onion

$^1/_3$ cup olive oil

4 tablespoons apple cider vinegar

Salt and pepper to taste

Briefly steam the broccoli pieces until tender, but with some crunch left. In boiling salted water, cook the potatoes until just tender. Drain. Put the potatoes and broccoli in a mixing bowl, and while still steaming, combine with rest of ingredients. Chill.

Serves 6

Vegetable Fish Chowder

1 cup chopped onions

2 cloves garlic, minced

3 tablespoons butter or vegetable oil

$^1/_2$ cup finely chopped fennel (from the bulb portion)

2 carrots, chopped

1 stalk celery, chopped

2 large potatoes, cubed

2 small white turnips, cubed

$^3/_4$ cup chopped green pepper

3 cups vegetable stock or water

$^3/_4$ teaspoon dried dill

$^1/_2$ teaspoon oregano

1 bay leaf

Salt and pepper to taste

$1^1/_2$ pounds any type or combination of firm, white fish fillets (e.g., cod, flounder, halibut, etc.), cut into 2-inch pieces (they will break up further as they cook and flake, but don't let them get too shredded)

$^3/_4$–1 cup light cream, half-and-half, or whole milk

Sauté onions and garlic in butter or oil until onions are translucent. Add fennel, carrots, celery, potatoes, and turnips and sauté for 5–7 minutes. Add green peppers, stock or water, dill, oregano, bay leaf, and simmer 15 minutes, or until vegetables are tender. Add salt and pepper to taste, then the fish pieces. Simmer until fish is cooked, not more than 10 minutes (less if the family will be reheating the chowder). Add cream or milk; stir gently.

Serves 4–6

CHICKEN SOUP CHICKEN PIE

One process for making two time-honored comfort courses: a simple broth and a very old-fashioned pot pie.

4–5 pounds chicken pieces

1 tablespoon salt

1 large white, or 2 medium yellow, onions, roughly chopped

1 stalk celery, cut into 1-inch pieces

1 carrot, cut into 1-inch slices

3 tablespoons oil or butter

4 tablespoons flour

8 cups chicken stock reserved, divided into 6-cup and 1-cup amounts

^{1}/4 cup heavy cream (coconut milk may be substituted)

^{1}/3 cup Sauterne

^{1}/4 teaspoon paprika

^{1}/8 teaspoon nutmeg

Salt and pepper to taste

2 frozen pie crusts, slightly defrosted, unbaked

3 cups roughly torn escarole

1^1/2 cups any little round *cooked* pasta: acine di pepe, pastina, even alphabet noodles if the household has small children

In stockpot, put chicken pieces, 1 tablespoon salt, onions, celery, and carrot. Barely cover with cold water, bring to boil, and simmer slowly, about 1–2 hours, or until chicken falls off the bone. Let everything cool in the stock. Skim fat thoroughly. Strain stock and set aside 2 cups for the next step—the remaining stock (or 6 cups of it) will be the base for the escarole soup.

Slip meat from bones in substantial pieces, discarding skin. Heat oil or butter, blend in flour, then gradually add the 2 cups stock, whisking and cooking until thickened. Add cream or coconut milk and Sauterne, and return onions, carrot, and celery to sauce. Season with paprika, nutmeg, and salt and pepper.

Cutting one of the pie crusts into appropriate strips, line the sides (not the bottom) of a deep-dish 9-inch pie pan. Lay the slices of white meat on the bottom of pan, and add enough dark meat slices to come halfway up sides of pan. Pour on the cream/vegetable sauce. Take the remaining whole pie crust and lay it over sauce and chicken, pressing and pinching its edges against the rim of the pie pan. Cut or pierce steam vents in the dough. Bake on middle rack for 20–25 minutes, or until golden brown.

Don't forget the soup. Bring 6 cups of reserved stock to a simmer, add the escarole, simmer it until the leaves wilt, and toss in the cooked pasta.

Serves 4–6

SWEET AND SOUR MEATBALLS WITH SALSA

Make this piquant variation on an old favorite a day ahead. Deliver with a baggie of boiled broad egg noodles. When sending pre-cooked pasta, always under-cook it just a touch, rinse thoroughly with cold water, drain, and toss with a little oil. If there are teenagers in the house, send this dish with hoagie rolls.

2 eggs

3 tablespoons ketchup

3 pounds ground beef or ground turkey (or combination)

2/3 cup matzoh meal or bread crumbs

1 can (16-oz.) whole cranberry sauce

1 cup (16-oz.) pineapple chunks or crushed pineapple in its own no-sugar-added juice. Do not drain.

1 jar (11.5-oz.) mild salsa

1 cup tomato sauce

Preheat oven to 350 degrees. Beat together eggs and ketchup. Combine thoroughly with ground meat and matzoh meal or crumbs. Form into balls. Place on baking sheet or broiler pan and bake 10–15 minutes.

Combine cranberry sauce, pineapple, salsa, and tomato sauce in large pot. Simmer gently for 5 minutes. Carefully add meatballs and simmer for 45 minutes or until cooked through.

Serves 6

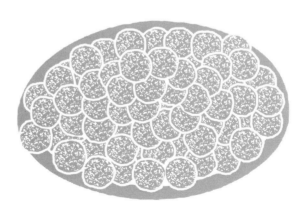

CHICK-PEA CURRY WITH MUSHROOMS AND ALMONDS

A lovely one-dish meal for a vegetarian family. (The Cheddar Broccoli Potato Salad (p. 60), a side dish for meat-eaters, also makes a good vegetarian main course.)

2 large onions, chopped

2 tablespoons canola oil

1 pound mushrooms, sliced (any variety or combination of varieties)

4 teaspoons ground cumin

1 can (28-oz.) crushed tomatoes

1 can (15-oz.) chick-peas, undrained

1 teaspoon ground coriander

1 teaspoon turmeric

1–2 teaspoons salt or to taste

$1/2$ teaspoon ground ginger

2 or 3 shakes Tabasco Sauce

$1/2$ cup slivered almonds, toasted (or sautéed in a little butter if the family uses milk products)

Sauté chopped onions in oil for 3 minutes. Add mushrooms and cumin and cook until both vegetables are soft. Add all remaining ingredients (except almonds) and simmer for at least 20 minutes, or until much of the liquid evaporates. Garnish with toasted almonds. Excellent over Basmati or any other kind of rice.

Serves 6

POTATO CARROT KUGEL

¹/₄ cup peanut oil, divided (vegetable oil may be substituted)

2 cups chopped onion

²/₃ cup finely grated carrot

2 pounds russet potatoes, peeled and coarsely grated

4 eggs, beaten

Salt and pepper to taste

Preheat oven to 400 degrees. In 2 tablespoons oil, sauté onions until golden. When onions are half-done, add finely grated carrots to wilt. Combine this mixture with the potatoes, eggs, and salt and pepper.

Use the remaining oil to generously coat a 13 x 9 x 2-inch Pyrex or gratin pan. Pour the potato mixture into pan, and bake in top third of oven for 50 minutes, or until top is golden and slightly crisp. As this dish bakes, it releases its oil, which you may use to baste the kugel once or twice.

Serves 8

CHALLAH

Many bakeries sell a braided bread they call challah; some are even pretty decent. But challah, to truly give you a taste of The World To Come, is best homemade.

Whether grieving or celebrating, Jews bless and eat this traditionally braided bread Friday night and Saturday. So although we include it in this sober chapter, please do not hesitate to give your Jewish loved ones challah on any Sabbath throughout the year (except Passover!). And if the mourners (or celebrants) are not Jewish, this beautifully-slicing egg bread is wonderful any day of the week.

2 packets (2^1/4 teaspoons each) active dry yeast

2^1/2 cups warm water

^{1}/3 cup sugar

2 teaspoons salt

^{1}/3 cup vegetable oil

4 eggs

8–9 cups flour, reserving about ^{1}/2 cup for flouring hands and work surface

Egg wash: 1 egg yolk beaten with 1 teaspoon water

Optional: **4 teaspoons poppy seeds or sesame seeds**

In very large bowl, dissolve yeast in warm water. Add sugar, salt, oil, 4 eggs, and 6 cups of the flour. Beat thoroughly. Gradually add flour until dough is stiff. Turn out dough onto work surface and knead until smooth and no longer sticky.

Place dough in large, lightly-oiled bowl, and cover with plastic wrap or a dish towel. Place in warm or breeze-free spot; let rise 1^1/2 hours. Punch down, divide into 4 portions, and braid (see diagram).

Place each of the 4 braided loaves in its own well-oiled loaf pan, or diagonally side-by-side on oiled baking sheets, 2 loaves to a sheet. Let rise about 1 hour, or until doubled in bulk.

Preheat oven to 375 degrees. Gently brush tops of loaves with the egg wash, and if desired, sprinkle with seeds. Bake for 30 minutes, or just until golden brown and hollow-sounding when tapped on bottom. Cool on racks.

Makes 4 loaves

HOW TO BRAID CHALLAH

1. For each loaf, divide its dough into three equal pieces.

2. Roll out each piece into long uniform strands. The pieces should be a bit longer than the pan in which the challah will be baked. Place the three strands side by side.

3. You will be braiding from the center down, then from the center up. Start at the center: Take the strand on the outer right and cross it over the middle strand to bring it into the middle.

4. Take the strand on the outer left, cross it over the middle strip and let it rest in the middle.

5. Repeat this procedure, alternately bringing the one on the outer right to the middle, and then bringing the strand on the outer left to the middle, working your way to the bottom.

6. Reverse the loaf so free ends point downward and finish braiding in the same manner. Tuck ends under to finish.

WHOLE WHEAT SOURDOUGH *BOULES*

Those earthen, chewy round loaves, but with a bit more fiber and vitamins—plus all the tang of sourdough without the headache of "starters."

1¹/₂ cups warm water

1 cup low-fat yogurt and its liquid, brought to room temperature

1 packet (2¹/₄ teaspoons) active dry yeast

6 cups whole wheat flour

1 tablespoon salt

Cornmeal

Spray-bottle of water

Combine water and yogurt. Stir in yeast until dissolved. Add 3 cups flour and beat until smooth. Add salt, then the remaining 3 cups flour, cup by cup, beating energetically.

Knead dough *while in bowl* until it is no longer sticky. Turn out onto floured work surface and knead, adding extra flour if dough needs additional stiffness. Place dough in clean, oiled bowl, cover with plastic wrap or dish towel, place in warm location, and let rise 1¹/₂ to 2 hours or until doubled in bulk. Punch down, and divide dough in half.

Grease 2 baking sheets and dust them with cornmeal. Shape dough into 2 plump, round loaves. Place a loaf on each sheet, and let rise in warm place until doubled in bulk.

Preheat oven to 400 degrees. Make very shallow diagonal slashes or cross-hatches in the top of each loaf. Spray the loaves lightly with water and bake 20 minutes. Open the oven door, spray loaves once more, close door, and continue baking another 20 minutes, or until bread sounds hollow when tapped.   *Makes 2 loaves*

CHOCOLATE GINGERBREAD

A melding of two childhood favorites, deliver this old-fashioned recipe with a quart of vanilla ice cream.

1 cup light molasses

$^1/_2$ cup buttermilk

1 tablespoon grated orange zest

1 tablespoon grated fresh ginger

1 teaspoon ground cinnamon

$^1/_8$ teaspoon ground cloves

$^1/_2$ teaspoon salt

2 ounces unsweetened baking chocolate

$^1/_2$ stick unsalted butter

1 teaspoon baking soda dissolved in 1 teaspoon water

2 cups whole wheat flour

1$^1/_2$ tablespoons pearl sugar*

Preheat oven to 375 degrees. Grease and flour a 9 x 9 x 2-inch baking pan. In large bowl, mix together molasses, buttermilk, orange zest, ginger, cinnamon, cloves, and salt. In microwave or double-boiler, melt chocolate and butter, then stir into buttermilk batter. Stir in baking soda and water mixture. Fold in flour.

Pour into pan and sprinkle with pearl sugar. Bake approximately 30 minutes or until center is set. Cool. If sending to another household, do not pre-slice. Remove from pan and wrap in foil. They can cut portions as desired, preventing staleness. *Makes 12 squares*

*Pearl or coarse sugar is available in most fine supermarkets in the baking aisle. It's also a nice choice for decorating the following recipe.

No-Roll Rich Sugar Cookies

All the early childhood sweetness, plus some extra adult richness—but no rolling pin, cookie cutters, or adhering dough.

4 cups sifted all-purpose flour

1 teaspoon baking powder

$1/2$ teaspoon baking soda

$1/2$ teaspoon salt

$1/4$ teaspoon nutmeg

$1/4$ teaspoon cinnamon

2 sticks butter, at room temperature

$1^1/2$ cups granulated sugar

1 egg

$1/2$ cup sour cream

1 teaspoon vanilla

$1/4$ cup pearl or granulated sugar

Optional: **slivered almonds, golden raisins**

Preheat oven to 375 degrees. Lightly grease cookie sheets. Sift flour with baking powder, soda, salt, nutmeg, and cinnamon. In mixing bowl, beat butter, sugar, and egg until fluffy. Add sour cream and vanilla, and beat until batter is smooth. Gradually add flour mixture, beating between additions. Divide dough into 4 balls, wrap in waxed paper, and refrigerate overnight or at least 2 hours.

Working with one ball at a time, break off pieces of dough to make small balls—each of the 4 portions should make about one dozen cookies. Place on cookie sheet 2 inches apart, and flatten with the bottom of a glass which you have dipped in flour. Sprinkle with either of the sugars, and/or the optional almonds or raisins. Bake 10–12 minutes or until golden. Cool on rack.   *Makes 48 cookies*

STRAWBERRIES IN FRESH ORANGE JUICE AND PORT

3 cups strawberries, washed and hulled

1–2 tablespoons sugar

2 large oranges, juiced

3/4 cup port

In the dish in which you will deliver them, sprinkle berries with sugar. Pour over the juice, and marinate 2 hours, gently stirring once. Add port. Plain, *serves 4*. Over pound cake, ice cream, or frozen yogurt, *serves 6–8*.

After the Funeral Food for a Crowd

More often than not, when there is an after-funeral meal to be planned, calls are made to the local delicatessen and orders are placed for large platters of fish, cheese, or meats and baskets full of fresh breads and rolls. Few people spend hours in the kitchen when their time is better spent comforting the bereaved. For this reason we are offering just a smattering of dessert-type finger foods that add sweetness to the table and the palate, and can be baked the night before.

Don't forget about sandwiches. Easy to prepare and easy to eat, tuna, egg salad, or chicken-salad sandwiches are always crowd-pleasers. Bring a tray heaped with sandwiches made on your favorite bread or rolls. They will be much appreciated as will a large tray of veggies with dip.

EVERYONE-ALREADY-KNOWS-THE-RECIPE SPINACH DIP

1 package (10-oz.) frozen chopped spinach (thawed and drained of all water)

1 envelope Knorr's instant vegetable soup mix

1 cup sour cream (low- or nonfat works well)

1 cup mayonnaise (low- or nonfat also works well)

1 cup plain yogurt

Mix all ingredients and chill overnight. Serve with crudités.

PHYLLIS' STRUDEL

1 can (13.5-oz.) Wondra flour

1 1/2 cups orange juice

1 1/2 cups vegetable oil

2 teaspoons baking soda

2 heaping teaspoons baking powder

2 teaspoons vanilla

2 jars (15-oz. each) apricot preserves

2 jars (15-oz. each) peach preserves

1/2 cup sugar

2 teaspoons ground cinnamon

1 cup chopped walnuts

Preheat oven to 350 degrees. Mix together flour, orange juice, oil, baking soda, baking powder, and vanilla. Divide dough into 6 pieces. Roll out each piece until dough begins to tear. Spread a generous amount of apricot and peach preserves onto dough. Mix sugar with ground cinnamon. Sprinkle on top of preserves. Sprinkle walnuts over. Roll up gently and place 2 rolls on a non-stick cookie sheet. Sprinkle again with sugar and cinnamon mixture. Bake for 30 minutes. Cool and slice. Repeat with remaining 4 rolls. You may have peach and apricot preserves left over.

Makes 36–50 slices

FROSTED PUMPKIN BARS

BARS:

2 cups flour

1 teaspoon baking soda

2 teaspoons baking powder

1 teaspoon cinnamon

2 cups sugar

1 cup vegetable oil

4 eggs

2 cups pumpkin

FROSTING:

1 package (3-oz.) cream cheese

³/4 stick butter

3 cups confectioners' sugar

1 tablespoon milk

Preheat oven to 350 degrees. Sift together flour, baking soda, baking powder, and cinnamon. Set aside.

Mix the sugar, oil, eggs, and pumpkin until smooth. Add the dry ingredients. Pour batter into a 12 x 18 x 2-inch greased pan and bake for 20–25 minutes.

While cake is cooling, beat together all of the frosting ingredients. Spread on cooled cake. Cut into bars.   *Makes 20 bars*

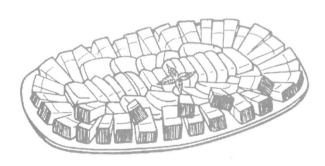

DATE NUT BARS

1 package (8-oz.) pitted dates, chopped

1 cup chopped raisins

1 cup chopped walnuts

1 teaspoon grated orange peel

1¹/₂ teaspoons cinnamon

1 cup sugar

1 stick butter at room temperature

1 teaspoon vanilla

2 eggs

2 cups all-purpose flour

2 teaspoons baking powder

¹/₂ teaspoon salt

2 tablespoons orange juice

Confectioners' sugar

Preheat oven to 375 degrees. Grease 2 baking sheets and set aside. In a large bowl, stir dates, raisins, walnuts, orange peel, cinnamon, and ¹/₂ cup sugar until fruit is coated with sugar. Set aside. In a a separate bowl, cream the butter with the remaining ¹/₂ cup sugar and vanilla until light and fluffy. Beat in eggs one at a time, mixing well after each addition. Stir in flour, baking powder, salt, and orange juice. Add to date mixture. Stir until blended. Do not overmix. Dough will be very stiff.

Divide dough into 4 portions. Shape 2 logs on each prepared baking sheet. Make logs about 12 x 2 x ¹/₂ inches. Bake 15 minutes. Although they turn slightly brown, logs will feel very soft and underdone. They will become firm as they cool. Cool 15 minutes. Cut diagonally into ³/₄-inch bars. Dust with confectioners' sugar. The bars freeze beautifully, *but dust with sugar only after defrosting.*

Makes about 60 bars

A Final Thought on Food and Death

Three days after the death of the 19-year-old, her mother Joann told us something "funny" as we watched her climb into her car. We will quote her directly: "I can't think. I can't move. I can't live. I didn't believe I would ever go anywhere again. Or get into a car, or go to a store. But we ran out of toilet paper!"

This was one of the greatest life lessons we've ever received. Even in the midst of the unspeakable, food must go in and out.

P.S. All the advice and recipes contained in this chapter apply equally to Birth.

8 Bowled Over
What to Bring to a Potluck

Out of comradeship can come and will come the happy life for all.
—Heywood Broun

There are many reasons to throw a potluck dinner. A new family moves into the neighborhood or an old family moves out. Your church has a fundraiser. The community theater production of "The King and I" is having their cast party.

Then again, sometimes the sun shines in Rochester, New York. It happened last year on May 25. Well! All the residents of the Cornhill area had not seen each other since before the long winter had begun the previous August. They threw open their windows, aired their goosedown comforters, washed their thermals, and walked, without crutches, into the middle of the street, now that most of their ice-induced injuries had healed. Was there a better reason for a potluck?

But Cornhill had learned its lesson. The Clothesline Arts Festival was held yearly nearby, and most of Rochester flocked to it. Last year the Cornhill denizens thought it would be nice to throw a potluck following an afternoon perusing the local Manets and Hockneys. Here's who brought what.

Tillie and Sam: Low-fat Lasagna

Maria and Charles: Lasagna with Sausage and Ground Meat

Veronica and Inge: Tuna Lasagna with Béchamel Sauce

Ron and Thor: Beef and Ale Lasagna

Joe: Hungry Pig Frozen Lasagna

Solstice and Rainforest Rubin: Organic Whole Wheat Vegetarian Tofu Lasagna

The Constantine Family: Deep Dish Broccoli Rabe and Jarlsburg Lasagna

Edna: Lasagna

Soooooooo … This year they elected Thor Chairperson of the Annual Cornhill Potluck Dinner Committee. In fact, Thor *was* the committee. That's what he got for not showing up at the election!

Thor was a model of administrative zeal, making certain not to assign Solstice and Rainforest the desserts. Instead he suggested they were born to bring the salads. When Maria and Charles offered to bring their Lasagna with Sausage and Ground Meat, he informed them the Constantine Family had already gotten dibs on Lasagna. Thor asked Maria and Charles, since the Constantine Lasagna was meatless, if they could just hold the noodles and bring a sausage casserole.

What they served …

All these recipes are true potluck treasures: They can be made up to two days ahead or frozen, and they serve 10–12 or more, depending on how many different dishes are on the menu. Except for one recipe (guess), they can either stand at room temperature losing their chill or heat without compromising the dish or they can be kept hot for hours and only improve. So also call on these recipes for buffets, chronically late guests, a family who eats in shifts, or for those times when the only thing you want to do on the day of your company meal is wash your hair.

TILLIE'S LOWISH-FAT CURRIED CHEESE ROLLS

2 pounds sharp, low-fat Cheddar cheese, grated

6 ounces low-fat cream cheese (Neufchâtel) at room temperature

2 cups pecans, chopped (coarsely if using a food processor, finely if combining recipe by hand) and very lightly toasted

3–4 cloves garlic, minced

6 shakes of Tabasco Sauce (less or more to taste)

Curry powder

Combine everything *except the curry powder* in your food processor and combine well without over-processing. Roll into 1-inch cylinders of almost the same length of the platter on which it will be served. Roll in curry powder.

Wrap in waxed paper and refrigerate overnight or at least 3 hours. Slices nicely for round crackers of any kind.

Serves Rochester. So if you are not making this for a potluck, halve the recipe, or put extra logs in the freezer *without rolling them in curry powder until they are defrosted (overnight in the fridge) and ready to serve.*   *Serves many*

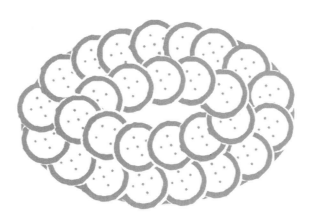

Sam's Convenience Food Tarts

Intentionally tacky title for elegant appetizer. One of the great cheats in our repertoire.

1 refrigerated pie crust package (each 15-oz. package contains 2 crusts)

2 cans (7.5-oz. each) Giovanni's Caponata*

1/4 cup fresh basil, finely chopped

1 1/2 cups shredded Gruyère cheese

3 cups heavy cream

6 eggs

Salt and pepper to taste

1–4 dashes of Tabasco Sauce, to taste

Preheat oven to 425 degrees. Press slightly softened crusts into two 9-inch tart pans with removable bottoms. (Sam, not being so *fency-shmency*, used a ceramic quiche dish and a disposable pie plate, and so can you.) Fold over outer circumference of dough, pressing to form a double thickness around the sides. Pierce the surfaces of the crusts with a fork and bake 10 minutes. Cool.

Reduce oven to 350 degrees. Spread 1 can of Caponata over *each* cooled crust. Sprinkle with basil, then with cheese. In bowl, whisk remaining ingredients together and pour 1/2 of the mixture over each Caponata-filled crust. Bake 20 minutes or until centers are no longer loose and quiches have puffed. Let sit for 5 minutes to set. May be served at any temperature. (If you got *fency*, don't forget to remove those pan sides.)

Each tart serves 8–10

*Caponata is Italian eggplant relish with olives and celery. It is available in specialty food stores and some supermarkets where, eerily, it changes aisles daily—from Ethnic Foods to Canned Vegetables to Gourmet Items. Equally mysterious, it is only available in those eensy-beensy cans.

LEMON SALAD À LA SOLSTICE

This unusual cooked and chilled salad can also be halved to create an invigorating summer luncheon course, or, with the addition of the best salami you can find, a simple supper. No matter what its destiny, this dish may be made up to 2 days ahead, and should be made 1 day ahead.

3 pounds tiny zucchini
1$\frac{1}{2}$ pounds ripe plum tomatoes
4 garlic cloves, minced
$\frac{1}{3}$ cup olive oil
$\frac{1}{4}$ cup fresh lemon juice
2 tablespoons fresh tarragon, minced
Pulp of 2 lemons
2 tablespoons scallions, minced

Cut zucchini into $\frac{3}{4}$-inch slices. Core tomatoes and cut into large dice. In skillet put zucchini, tomatoes, garlic, olive oil, lemon juice, and tarragon. Season to taste with salt and pepper, and mix well but gently. Bring to boil, then lower heat and simmer until zucchini are just tender; baby zucchini can take as little as 4 minutes. Remove from heat.

Get the lemon pulp out of your lemons any way you wish. Either peel and seed them, or scoop out the pulp with a serrated grapefruit spoon. Just make sure there are no seeds or bitter white rind. Chop the pulp finely and stir into the skillet mixture. Cool thoroughly and turn into serving bowl or onto concave platter. Garnish with scallions and chill until ready to serve. *Serves 10–12*

Rainforest's Marinated Organic Beets on Their Own Greens

Should be made a day ahead and assembled a few hours before serving.

7 pounds organic beets with their greens attached (smaller, younger beets are better, and if you can't find the organic, young beets are *essential*)

1/3 cup olive oil, plus 2 tablespoons

1/3 cup freshly squeezed orange juice

2 tablespoons honey

Pinch of salt and pepper

Bring a stockpot of water, with 1 or 2 teaspoons salt, to a boil. Meanwhile, leaving 1/2 inch of the stem attached to the beet, cut away the rest of the leafy beet greens. Wash and drain greens, removing the thicker stems, and set greens aside in a colander to drip-dry. (Beet stems may be saved for dark stocks and borscht, or chopped and used raw in salads.)

Scrub the beets, place in boiling water, and cook until fork tender. Depending on the size and age of your beets, this takes between 25 minutes and 1 hour at a true boil, not a simmer. Keep checking with that fork. Drain and slip off the skins by rubbing the beets under cold water. Cut the beets into chunks; if you obtained the small ones, simply quarter them. Put in bowl.

Whisk together 1/3 cup olive oil, orange juice, honey—and salt and pepper only if necessary. Pour over the still hot beets. Mix, cover, and chill. In skillet, heat 2 tablespoons olive oil, and sauté greens very briefly until wilted. Cover and chill in separate container.

Several hours before serving, line your platter with the greens, top with the marinated beets, and bring to room temperature. Or heat gently and serve warm.   *Serves 12–15*

CHARLES' SAUSAGE, CAULIFLOWER, AND ONION SKILLET

3 pounds mixed sweet and hot Italian sausage links

3 tablespoons olive oil

2 cauliflower heads, broken into florets, steamed for 3 minutes, and drained

4 onions, very coarsely chopped

2 tablespoons crushed fennel seeds

2 tablespoons dried basil

1 tablespoon fresh rosemary, chopped

1 teaspoon hot pepper flakes

5 cloves garlic, chopped

2 cups Chianti or other young red wine

2 tablespoons tomato paste thinned in 1 cup warm water

Optional: **aged balsamic vinegar**

In your largest skillet, brown and cook the sausages thoroughly on all sides. Cut into 1-inch chunks and place in the casserole or chafing dish in which you will serve the finished recipe. Remove fat from skillet, add the olive oil, and sauté the cauliflower until golden. Lift florets out with a slotted spoon and place them in your casserole.

In whatever oil remains in skillet, wilt the onions slightly. Add remaining ingredients (except vinegar), stir, cover, and simmer 10–15 minutes. Dump this mixture over the sausage and cauliflower. Mix well, and keep on hot tray or over flame in chafing dish. If desired, drizzle sparingly at this point with aged balsamic vinegar. *Serves 10–12*

The Constantine Family's Broccoli Rabe-Jarlsburg Lasagna

6 cups good jarred or homemade pasta sauce

1^1/2–2 pounds imported Italian lasagna noodles, cooked according to package directions

2 bunches broccoli rabe, chopped, and sautéed briefly until just wilted

1 cup walnuts, chopped and lightly toasted

2 cups cottage cheese

1^1/3 cups fresh, shaved (not grated) Parmesan

24 slices of Jarlsburg cheese

Preheat oven to 350 degrees. In deep-dish lasagna pan, spread 1^1/2 cups of the sauce. Then ^{1}/3 of: noodles, broccoli rabe, walnuts, cottage cheese, Parmesan shavings, and a layer of Jarlsburg slices. Layer two more times, ending with sauce, nuts, and cheeses. May be frozen or refrigerated at this point.

When ready to serve or bring to potluck, bake for 50 minutes to 1 hour. Check to see if the center is piping hot. If the cheese and nuts are browning too quickly, or the corners are drying and curling, cover with foil. Let sit at least 10 minutes to set. This is pretty pre-sliced on the diagonal into about 12–16 diamonds, and much easier for buffet service.*   *Serves 10–12*

A note about lasagnas and potlucks: The authors are frankly mystified as to why everyone other than they believe lasagna to be the perfect buffet main course. If kept on a hot tray, it dries out and the edges harden. If not kept hot, the cheese congeals and the whole laborious thing looks like Silly Putty. But we included it here because people doing potlucks always request lasagna recipes from us … maybe they know something we don't. Anyway, Thor made us.

We prefer to serve it fresh from the oven to our families or at small dinner parties. After some simple antipasti, before the espresso, and along with its trite but perfect garlic bread sidekick, we predict a comeback for this honorable and filling dish in all its variations.

Maria's Contribution

Maria went to the best bakery in Rochester and loaded up on the round and **long crusty French and Italian loaves** that would go so well with Charles' sausage, the Constantines' lasagna, and the Rubins' salads. She set them out in a huge basket with cutting boards and bread knives handy, so neighbors could help themselves. Alongside she placed bowls of **butter**, **lebnah** (see page 130), and **Oregano Oil**.

Oregano Oil

Potlucks and other large gatherings bring out a community's idiosyncratic dietary profile. It is considerate (and no sweat at all) to set out a no-animal-products bread and veggie dip for those who are dairy-sensitive, kosher non-dairy for that particular meal, or vegan. For the same reasons, it is also thoughtful to set out a platter of raw vegetables and a bowl of fruit.

This elemental but celestial oil must be prepared at least a week in advance. Decant into a pretty cup and present with a new 1-inch paint brush. Endlessly multiply the recipe to have some on hand for your own sauté oil, salad dressing base, and holiday gift purposes.

1 cup wonderful olive oil
$^1/_2$ cup perfect fresh oregano, washed and dried

Immerse a 1-cup jelly, canning, or glass jar and its lid in boiling water to sterilize. Remove from water, and while the jar is still hot, put in the two ingredients and cover tightly. Place in a cool, dark area for 8–12 days.

Did you think you could get away without having a bean dish at a potluck? Better luck next time! Thor assigned a cold one and a hot one. Lucky for us Inge was able to step outside the standard potluck conceit.

INGE'S TOO-GOOD-FOR-A-POTLUCK BAKED BEANS IN COGNAC AND THYME

1 stick butter

2 large onions, chopped

1 large can (12-oz.) tomato paste

Reserved liquid from beans combined with enough water to make 1^1/2 cups total liquid

^{1}/2 cup chopped, fresh parsley or basil

1 cup dry red wine

^{1}/2 cup cognac

3 whole cloves garlic

1 teaspoon dried thyme

2 bay leaves

Salt and pepper to taste

3 cans (1 lb. 3-oz. each) white beans, drained with their liquid saved
(Purists and others who do not live Actual Real Lives may make 3^1/2 pounds of dried white beans from scratch if they wish, but it is unnecessary for this transformational recipe.)

Preheat oven to 325 degrees. In large saucepan, melt butter and sauté chopped onion until translucent. Add rest of ingredients except for beans. Simmer 15–25 minutes, or until thickened and reduced slightly. Add beans and combine thoroughly.

Grease a large bean pot, Dutch oven, or covered casserole with olive oil. Add bean mixture. Cover tightly and bake 1^1/2 hours. Remove bay leaves. Serve hot, but don't get frantic as it cools down; these are the kind of beans binge-eaters eat cold from the fridge with their hands.   *Serves 10–12*

GAIL'S GUACAMOLE AND BEAN LAYERED SPREAD

The guacamole component all on its lonesome is excellent; the complete dish is a favorite potluck and party munchie.

GUACAMOLE:

3 ripe avocados

$1/2$ small onion, minced

1 ripe tomato, cored and finely chopped

1 pickled jalapeño pepper, minced

1 clove garlic, pressed

10 sprigs fresh cilantro, chopped

$1/2$ teaspoon salt

$1/2$ lime, juiced

ADDITIONAL INGREDIENTS:

1 container (16-oz.) sour cream

1 envelope (1.25-oz.) taco seasoning mix

2 cans (16-oz. each) refried beans (with or without green chiles, but better with them)

2 cups grated Cheddar cheese

2 ripe tomatoes, seeded, cored, finely chopped

4–5 scallions, chopped

$1/2$ cup thinly sliced pitted black olives

Tortilla chips

Cut avocados in half lengthwise. Remove pits and reserve. Scrape out meat with spoon into bowl and mash. Add rest of Guacamole ingredients and combine thoroughly. Return pits to mixture; cover with plastic wrap, pressing wrap directly onto mixture.

In small bowl, combine sour cream and taco mix. On a 10- to 12-inch flat round serving platter, spread refried beans, leaving room on circumference of platter for what will be a final border of tortilla chips. Remove pits from guacamole and spread mixture on top of beans, leaving a narrow border of bean layer showing. Next spread sour cream mixture, leaving a border of guacamole showing. Sprinkle top with cheese, tomatoes, scallions, and olives. Surround entire recipe with a tortilla chip border (putting rest of chips in basket).   *Serves 10–12*

What Joe Brought

What to do when you're forbidden to bring your beloved Hungry Pig Frozen Lasagna? Joe called Thor cruel names and sulked. Then he ran to the mother of one of the authors and begged for this recipe. When Hilda's Rhubarb Compote is on the buffet, folks eat it first as an appetizer, then as a relish with the main course, and finally as a dessert. In fact, they often stand by the serving dish, asocial and careless of appearance, shoveling it into their faces with the serving ladle.

Hilda's Rhubarb Compote

1 pound package frozen cut rhubarb

1 pound package frozen whole strawberries without syrup or sugar

4 large peeled Macintosh apples, cut into chunks

1 whole large navel orange, unpeeled, sliced thin

4 or 5 ripe peaches, cut into chunks

1 cup sugar

Hilda: "Combine everything in a saucepan and cook on low flame until the consistency of coarse applesauce. Add a cup of sugar. Or more. To taste. Stir through. Cook another five minutes. Chill very well and serve. Can you make it in advance? Days. You can put it in your freezer and forget it's there and give it to people for Thanksgiving instead of cranberry sauce and they'll kiss your hands.

"Caution: This 'gameszha'* loves to dirty your stove. Just when you think it is solidly down in the bottom of your pan, it boils over, and you have a sticky red stove-top; you and your burners are never again the same. So have it in mind.

"Also, if you have any suicidal fruit in the house, you can throw it in."   *Serves 10–12*

"Gameszha" is a faux-Yiddish word meaning "mixture" or "mess o,' " as in "gameszha o' greens." At least we believe it to be faux. If the reader knows differently please contact the publisher.

PHYLLIS' PEACH PIE

Since guests have been known to pass up the baked goods in favor of the previous compote, Joe had no choice but to bring dessert from the only cook equal to Hilda's genius: the other author's mother. Make several of these pies. Horde one.

$^1/_2$ cup light brown sugar

$^3/_4$ cup sifted flour

1 stick butter

One 9-inch purchased or homemade pic crust, unbaked

2 pounds ripe peaches, peeled and quartered

$^1/_2$ cup white sugar

$^1/_2$ teaspoon nutmeg or cinnamon

1 egg

2 tablespoons cream

1 teaspoon vanilla

Preheat oven to 400 degrees. In small bowl, combine brown sugar and flour. Cut in butter to create streusel. Sprinkle $^1/_2$ cup of streusel on unbaked crust. Arrange peaches on streusel.

Combine white sugar with nutmeg or cinnamon and sprinkle over peaches. Beat egg, cream, and vanilla, and pour over sugared peaches. Top with remaining streusel. Bake 40–50 minutes, or until top is brown.

Each pie serves 6–8

EDYE'S CHOCOLATE STRAWBERRY TART

*Double this divine creation to have enough for your crowd. Worth the effort if you truly want 'em …
bowled over.*

CRUST:

1^1/2 cups flour

3 tablespoons sugar

^{1}/2 teaspoon salt

**9 tablespoons butter, chilled
and cut into pieces**

2 egg yolks

1 teaspoon vanilla

1 teaspoon lemon juice

1 teaspoon water

Sift flour, sugar and salt into large bowl. Using pastry blender, fingertips, or food processor, work butter pieces into dry ingredients until mixture resembles coarse cornmeal. Work quickly to avoid warming dough.

In separate bowl, whisk remaining crust ingredients together. Add to dough, and pulse-process until dough begins to form ball (or stir with fork until dough can be shaped into ball). With hands and work surface floured, knead dough until it no longer adheres to hands—this should only take 4 or 5 kneads. Reshape to ball, and flatten between 2 pieces of waxed paper to form a disk. Cover and refrigerate 30 minutes to 2 hours.

Preheat oven to 425 degrees. Working quickly, roll out dough between waxed paper to form a round large enough to cover bottom and sides of 8- to 9-inch tart pan. (*Options: a tart pan with removable sides, a springform pan, or a fluted-edge pie or quiche pan.*) Lay dough in pan, press dough into sides. Trim off excess dough leaving enough extra to turn over and create a decorative edge.

Line the dough with foil, and weight with beans, rice, or pie weights. Bake 8 minutes. Remove weights and foil. Prick crust surface with a fork. Return to oven until edges are browned, about 8–10 minutes longer. Cool in pan, on rack. *continued on next page*

FILLING:

1 cup high quality semisweet chocolate pieces

2 tablespoons unsalted butter, melted

3 tablespoons cherry or coffee liqueur

$1/4$ cup confectioners' sugar, sifted

1 tablespoon water

TOPPING:

2 pints strawberries, washed, stemmed, hulled, and dried. Strawberries should be as close to perfect as possible, in color, ripeness, and uniformity of size.

3 tablespoons red currant or apricot jelly

1 tablespoon cherry liqueur

FILLING: Melt chocolate in double boiler. When chocolate has softened, add melted butter and liqueur. Whisk until completely blended and smooth. Add sugar and water; continue whisking. Pour into cooled tart shell.

TOPPING: While filling is warm, place berries in a circular pattern starting at the outer edge. Melt jelly with liqueur until glaze is pourable. Slowly pour glaze over berries, coating them all well. Refrigerate at least 2 hours. Remove $1/2$ hour before serving. (This step is unnecessary for a potluck or any other buffet where food is sitting out for extended periods.) If you used a tart pan with removable sides, remove, and place tart, still on tart pan bottom, on larger platter.

One tart serves 8–10

Ron and Thor's Contribution

Beer and ale. A selection of sodas and bottled waters. A bowl of lemon and lime wedges. Two huge jugs of inexpensive wine no one drank except Thor; administration does that to a person.

EDNA'S OVERNIGHT BOURBON BURGUNDY GLÖGG

Edna, however, sick unto death of the neighborhood politely ignoring her, had a little something up her sleeve.

1¹/2 pounds raisins (organic preferable)
3–4 cups water
1¹/4 cups sugar
1 cinnamon stick, broken into pieces
1 tablespoon whole cloves
2 tablespoons cardamom seeds
1 gallon good Burgundy
From ¹/2 to an entire quart of bourbon

Put raisins in stockpot and cover with water. Add sugar, cinnamon pieces, and cloves. Crack cardamom seeds open, and along with shells, add to pot. Bring to boil, then immediately lower heat, cover, and simmer for 2 or more hours—the raisins should be plumped and soft. You may have to add water. Remove from heat.

Add Burgundy, bring back to heat, and keep heating, just under a simmer, for an additional 2 hours. Cool overnight, leaving in all the fruit and spices. In the morning, drain, pressing hard on the raisins to extract their wine-y juices. If not serving that day, pour into sterilized bottles, cork, and refrigerate. When serving, reheat, add bourbon, and ladle into ceramic or glass mugs. For the potluck, Edna reheated it in the stockpot, added almost a whole quart of Jack Daniels, heated it a bit more, and poured it into thermoses.

"Let 'em think it's mousy little Edna's herb tea," she cackled. *40–50 servings*

LATER ...

The residents of Cornhill were thrilled there was no snow that day. They gratefully set up their tables in the freezing rain, and very happily ate from a wide variety of delicious food. The lovely herb tea was especially warming.

9 Eggs-Its
Breakfasts Before Saying Good-bye

A faithful friend is a strong defense, and he that findeth such findeth a treasure.
—Ben Sira

WinonaAndDebbie were so inseparable in high school they were inseparable.

So when it came time to apply to college, they based their selections solely on which institutions were so desperate for applicants they'd not only completely disregard SAT scores, but they'd allow one to pick one's own roommate. They applied to the American campus of Pol Pot University, Petticoat Junction Technical Institute, and the LA Freeway Correspondence Program, attended from one's automobile. The choice was practically made for them when the University of Antarctica announced their two-for-one sale.

WinonaAndDebbie bought their parkas together: one purple with a beige hood, one beige with a purple hood. WinonaAndDebbie majored in Engineering, minored in Political Eco-Anthropology of the Pacific Rim, and Debbie played basketball.

WinonaAndDebbie graduated with honors (at UA a 2.9), then rented an apartment together in Ft. Lauderdale where they attended graduate school and worked together as taffy pullers at a seaside amusement park. Debbie also played basketball.

One day, while stretching butterscotch taffy for the snowbirds, WinonaAndDebbie were interrupted by a woman who seemed to know Debbie.

To make a non-story short, the woman was a scout for the WNBA. She had visited UA during summer break, and had seen Debbie dribbling while executing a perfect triple Lutz on the still-frozen pond. But those were the days when women basketball players were just women playing basketball. Two years and two WNBA teams later, scouts were in hot pursuit: Men had figured out they could make money from women's basketball.

As Debbie packed and cried, trying to sort out her own clothes from Winona's, Winona cried and cooked breakfast, trying to divide their mutually-purchased kitchen utensils fairly. The least she could do was serve Debbie a hearty going-away breakfast.

WHAT TO SERVE?

Most people think of going-away food in the context of crowded cocktail, dinner, or dessert parties. The truth is, most people leave for wherever they're going, without much fanfare, after breakfast. A lovingly prepared morning meal will be both comforting and memorable for the person remaining behind as well as for the wayfarer.

SCRAMBLED EGGS WITH SCALLIONS, SMOKED FISH, AND TOMATOES

2 tomatoes, halved

6 large eggs

1/4 cup whole milk (do not substitute skim)

2 tablespoons butter

1 tablespoon chopped scallions

1/2 pound smoked bluefish, salmon, or trout skinned, boned and flaked

Salt and pepper to taste

Preheat broiler. Arrange tomatoes cut side up on baking sheet. Broil until lightly colored and tender, about 5 minutes. Season to taste with salt and pepper. Cover with foil to keep warm.

Whisk eggs with milk in large bowl. Season with salt and pepper.

Melt butter in heavy, nonstick skillet over low heat. Add egg mixture and cook until almost set, stirring frequently, about 5 minutes. Stir in scallions and remove from heat. Spoon eggs into center of large platter. Sprinkle with smoked fish and encircle the eggs with the tomatoes. *Serves 4*

LOW-FAT BAKED BANANA FRENCH TOAST

8 thin slices of your favorite light (reduced fat) bread

4 ripe bananas

1/2 cup skim milk

2 large eggs

1 teaspoon vanilla

Pinch of cinnamon

Confectioners' sugar

Raspberries for garnish

Pure maple syrup

Preheat oven to 350 degrees. With fork, mash a piece of banana into each of 4 slices of bread. Top each with a remaining bread slice. In a glass pie dish, whisk together milk, eggs, vanilla, and cinnamon. One at a time, dip each bread stack into egg mixture letting it soak for 45 seconds.

Spray large, nonstick skillet with vegetable oil spray. Heat over medium heat. Add French toast to the skillet and cook until golden, about 2 minutes per side. Transfer to greased or nonstick baking sheet and bake 8 minutes. Transfer to plates. Dust with confectioners' sugar and garnish with raspberries. Serve with maple syrup on the side.   *Serves 4*

BLINTZ SOUFFLÉ

2 packages (6 to a package) frozen cheese blintzes

1 stick butter, melted

5 beaten eggs

1 teaspoon vanilla

1/4 teaspoon salt

1/4 cup sugar

3/4 cup orange juice

3/4 cup sour cream

Preheat oven to 350 degrees. Place blintzes in large, greased baking dish. Blend all ingredients except sour cream. After blended, stir in sour cream. Pour mixture over frozen blintzes and bake 45 minutes or until the soufflé is puffed and brown.   *Serves 6*

VEGETABLE FRITTATA WITH HERBS AND GOAT CHEESE

1 tablespoon olive oil

4 small red bliss potatoes

1 medium onion, halved and thinly sliced

1 red bell pepper, julienned

1 yellow pepper, julienned

2 tablespoons chopped fresh basil

2 teaspoons minced fresh rosemary

1/4 teaspoon salt

8 large eggs

1 teaspoon dried dill

4 ounces chilled goat cheese

Olive oil spray

Salt and pepper to taste

Heat oil in large nonstick ovenproof skillet over medium-low heat. Add potatoes, onion, peppers, basil, rosemary, and salt. Cook 5 minutes stirring occasionally. Cover and cook until potatoes are tender, about 15 minutes, stirring occasionally. Cool mixture in skillet 5 minutes.

Preheat oven to 350 degrees. Whisk eggs and dill in large bowl. Season with salt and pepper. Mix in 3 ounces goat cheese. Set aside several potato slices and bell pepper strips. Stir remaining vegetable mixture into egg mixture.

Wipe skillet clean. Add oil and heat over medium-high heat. Pour egg and vegetable mixture into skillet, stirring vegetables to distribute evenly. Arrange reserved vegetables attractively on top. Sprinkle with 1 ounce goat cheese. Cook until sides of frittata begin to brown, about 2 minutes. Transfer skillet to oven and bake until frittata is set in center, about 15 minutes. Cut frittata into sections and serve.

Serves 4

German Apple (or Lemon) Pancake

This is one large, special pancake you cut and serve to your guests.

PANCAKE:

3 large eggs

3/4 cup milk

3/4 cup flour

1/2 teaspoon salt

Optional: **1/2 cup thin-sliced apples**

1 1/2 tablespoons butter

FILLING:

1 pound tart, fresh apples such as Granny Smith

1 stick melted butter

1/4 cup sugar

Dash cinnamon and nutmeg

TOPPING:

2 tablespoons melted butter

Confectioners' sugar

Preheat oven to 450 degrees. Beat together eggs, milk, flour, and salt until smooth. Add optional apples at this point, if desired. In a heavy 12-inch skillet, melt about 1 1/2 tablespoons butter. As soon as butter is hot, pour in batter and put skillet in oven. After 15 minutes lower oven temperature to 350 degrees and continue baking for another 10 minutes. Pancake should be light brown and crisp.

During the first 10 or 15 minutes of baking, the pancake may puff up in large bubbles. If this happens, pierce with a fork.

While pancake is baking, make filling. Peel and thinly slice the apples. Sauté in butter and add sugar. Season to taste with cinnamon and nutmeg. The apples should be tender but not too soft.

ASSEMBLY:

When pancake is ready, slide it onto a platter, pour apple filling over one side, and fold the other side over. Sprinkle with melted butter and confectioners' sugar and serve hot.

For a simpler, but equally delicious pancake, eliminate the filling completely and don't put any apples in the pancake batter. When the pancake is cooked, squeeze juice of 1/2 lemon over it, and sprinkle with confectioners' sugar.

Serves 6

BLUEBERRY BREAD

2 cups sugar

2 sticks butter or margarine

4 eggs

1 cup milk

5 cups flour (preferably 3 cups white and 2 cups wheat)

1 teaspoon salt

5 teaspoons baking powder

1 tablespoon cinnamon

4 tablespoons sugar

3 cups blueberries

Preheat oven to 350 degrees. Cream sugar and butter until completely mixed. Beat eggs into this mixture one at a time. Slowly add milk. In separate bowl, combine dry ingredients and stir well. Add small amounts of the milk mixture and flour mixture alternately, stirring after each addition and ending with the flour. Fold blueberries into batter. Pour batter into two well-greased loaf pans. Bake 45–50 minutes.

Makes 2 loaves

EGGS FLORENTINE

$^1/_2$ **pound shiitake mushrooms**

1 can (14-oz.) chicken broth

2 tablespoons butter, divided

1 package (10-oz.) ready-cut fresh spinach

$^1/_2$ **cup chopped onion**

2 tablespoons flour

2 tablespoons whipping cream

6 eggs

$^1/_3$ **cup grated Parmesan cheese**

Salt and pepper

Rinse mushrooms and pat dry. Bring broth to boil and pour over mushrooms. Let stand about 20 minutes. Melt 1 tablespoon butter in large skillet and add spinach. Cook until spinach is wilted. Arrange spinach in bottom of 9 x 13 x 2-inch baking dish.

Melt remaining 1 tablespoon butter in a medium saucepan and sauté onion until tender, about 4 minutes. Add flour and stir 1 minute. Gradually mix in mushrooms with broth and whipping cream. Boil, whisking constantly until sauce thickens, about 4 minutes. Season to taste with salt and pepper.

Preheat oven to 400 degrees. Without breaking yolks, crack eggs over spinach, spacing evenly. Spoon mushroom mixture around eggs leaving yolks exposed. Sprinkle with Parmesan, salt, and pepper. Bake until eggs are set, about 15 minutes. Serve with toast. *Serves 3*

LATER ...

Pulling taffy just wasn't the same with Gus, the new acne-ridden, hormone-infested teenager they hired to replace Debbie. It would take Winona some time to learn the ropes, joys, and benefits of not being WinonaAndDebbie. Debbie, on the other hand, was blissfully happy and wealthy.

And every year no matter what, Winona   and   Debbie held their annual breakfast reunion.

10 Mean Cuisine
Menus for Your Child's First Experience with Prejudice

We did not come over on the same ship, but we were all in the same boat.
—Bernard M. Baruch

Rachel came home from school silent and white-faced. Mrs. Goldfarb felt her daughter's head: no fever. "Ruchelah, my angel, do you want to tell me about it?"

Rachel winced at the sound of her diminutive. "This is America, Mommy. Don't ever call me that again." Tina Goldfarb knew this was America, as she and her family had lived in Danbury, Connecticut for three generations. She also now knew why Rachel was pale.

"Angel, who insulted you?"

"It doesn't matter."

"It always matters. Nothing matters more than hate and ignorance. This is a very old story, Rachel, and almost every Jewish child experiences it. I can't help you cope if you don't share what happened."

What happened was that a fifth grade classmate, Billy, made age-old use of recess by tossing a penny onto the blacktop right at Rachel Goldfarb's feet. "Pick it up you penny-pinching Jew."

WHAT TO SERVE?

SPECIAL BRISKET

5–6 pounds brisket

1–2 teaspoons flour

Black pepper

$1/4$ cup corn oil

8 onions, thickly sliced

2 tablespoons tomato paste

$1^1/2$ teaspoons salt

2 cloves garlic, quartered

6 carrots, divided

Preheat oven to 375 degrees. Trim fat from meat. Dust with flour and sprinkle with pepper. Heat oil in casserole. Add brisket and brown over medium-high heat on both sides until edges are crispy. Transfer meat to a dish. Add onions to casserole and stir. Cook 10–15 minutes until onions are brown. Remove casserole from heat. Add meat. Spread tomato paste over meat as if it were icing. Sprinkle with salt and pepper. Add garlic and 1 carrot and cover tightly. Bake $1^1/2$ hours. Remove from oven. Slice the brisket and reassemble it. Add water and 5 remaining carrots. Cover and bake $1^3/4$ to 2 hours longer.

Serves 10

BEST POTATO LATKES

6 Idaho potatoes

1 medium onion, grated

2 eggs

Salt and pepper

Flour as needed

Canola or olive oil: $1/4$ inch deep in large frying pan

Sour cream or applesauce

Peel potatoes and grate in food processor. Squeeze out as much water as possible from grated potatoes. Add grated onion, eggs, salt and pepper. Add flour one tablespoon at a time until mixture thickens slightly. Heat oil in pan over medium-high heat. Place large spoonfuls of potato mixture into oil and fry until golden brown on both sides. Drain on paper towels. Serve with sour cream or applesauce.   *Serves 8*

TRADITIONAL JEWISH CHICKEN SOUP

1 kosher chicken (4–5 pounds)

4 quarts cold water

2 to 3 stalks celery, including the leaves

1 large onion

1 parsnip, peeled

3 carrots, peeled

1 parsley root, peeled

1 piece celery knob

A few sprigs of fresh parsley and dill

Salt and white pepper to taste

Cut chicken into quarters; place in large pot with cold water to cover. Bring to boil, lower heat, and simmer one hour. Remove the scum as it rises.

Add all vegetables, salt, and pepper and cook for an additional hour or until chicken is tender when pierced with a fork. Remove chicken and vegetables; strain soup. Let soup cool so fat can be skimmed from the top. Heat to serve.

Serves 12

SPINACH JEWISH STYLE

3 pounds fresh spinach

Salt

$^1/_2$ cup dark, seedless raisins

1 cup lukewarm water

3 tablespoons olive oil

$^1/_2$ small onion, minced

$^1/_4$ cup pine nuts

Freshly ground black pepper

Dash nutmeg

Remove stems and roots from spinach. Rinse in at least three changes of cold water until all sand is removed. Place spinach in large saucepan with a pinch of salt and no water other than that retained from washing. Cover and cook over moderately high heat for 5 minutes. Drain.

Soak raisins in lukewarm water for 5 minutes. Drain.

Heat oil in large skillet. Add onion and sauté until soft and translucent. Add raisins, pine nuts, and small amounts of salt and pepper. Sauté, stirring, 1 minute. Add spinach and nutmeg and sauté, stirring frequently, until spinach looks dry and crisp.

Serves 6

BUBBE'S APPLE CAKE

4 cups apples, peeled and diced

2 cups sugar

1 cup chopped black walnuts

3 cups flour

$^1/_2$ teaspoon nutmeg or cinnamon

$^1/_2$ teaspoon salt

$^1/_2$ teaspoon baking soda

1 cup vegetable oil

1 teaspoon vanilla

2 eggs, well beaten

$^1/_4$ cup apple juice or Calvados or apple butter

Preheat oven to 325 degrees. Mix apples, sugar and nuts and let stand for 1 hour. In large bowl, mix together remaining ingredients, except apple juice, Calvados, or apple butter. When blended, add diced apple mixture and stir.

Bake in greased tube pan for 1$^1/_4$ hours. Cake should be dark brown when done.

When cake has cooled, brush with apple juice, Calvados, or apple butter.

Makes 1 tube cake

While Mrs. Tina Goldfarb told Rachel the actual statistics of charitable donations from Jews nation- and world-wide, she quickly rethought her dinner menu. She refroze the macaroni and cheese and defrosted last week's brisket and latkes.

Tina and all the mothers know that ethnic cuisine is the earliest, most immediate, and most visceral experience of positive cultural identity.

When Billy put bubble gum in Tasha Robinson's corn rows, snidely asked José Dominquez if his father had a green card, and insulted the shape of Jen Chang's beautiful eyes, all of their mothers refroze the macaroni and cheese.

MRS. ROBINSON'S SOUTHERN FRIED CHICKEN

One 3- to 4-pound chicken, cut into eighths

1 tablespoon salt

1 tablespoon sugar

1 teaspoon cornstarch

1 teaspoon black pepper

$1/4$ teaspoon garlic powder

$1^1/2$ cups flour

4 cups canola oil, divided

Wash chicken pieces and pat dry with paper towels. Combine next five ingredients in small dish. Sprinkle this mixture on all sides of each chicken piece. Dredge the pieces in the flour and shake off excess.

Working in two batches, heat 2 cups oil in deep skillet over medium-high heat. Add half the chicken. Carefully moving and turning the pieces, fry until golden brown, about 20 minutes. Repeat with second 2 cups of oil and rest of chicken.

Gently transfer to paper towels and drain. May be served immediately, at room temperature, or cold for a picnic.   *Serves 4*

SWEET POTATO PONE

6 medium sweet potatoes

$1/2$ stick butter or margarine or $1/4$ cup vegetable oil

2 cups sugar

3 eggs, beaten

$1/2$ teaspoon each: cinnamon, allspice, nutmeg, ground cloves

12 ounces white raisins

Preheat oven to 400 degrees. Bake sweet potatoes 1 hour and 10 minutes or until fork-tender. Peel, slice into thick rounds, and place in single layer in ovenproof dish. Cream butter and sugar. Add remaining ingredients to butter/sugar mixture and spread over the potatoes. Bake at 250 degrees for 1 hour.   *Serves 8–10*

TALLAHASSEE FUDGE PIE

1 stick butter

1 cup sugar

2 eggs

2 squares unsweetened chocolate, melted

¹/₄ cup flour

¹/₄ teaspoon salt

1 teaspoon vanilla

²/₃ cup chopped pecans

Vegetable oil spray

1 pint vanilla ice cream or frozen yogurt

Preheat oven to 350 degrees. Cream butter and sugar. Add eggs one at a time, thoroughly incorporating each one. Blend in chocolate. Add flour, salt, and vanilla. Mix very gently. Stir in pecans. Pour into 8-inch pie pan greased with cooking spray.

Bake for 20–25 minutes until edges are dry, but center is still moist. Cool. Serve warm or at room temperature, never chilled. Top with ice cream or yogurt. *Serves 6–8*

Mrs. Dominquez' Red Snapper

2 pounds red snapper fillets

Salt to taste

2 tablespoons lime juice

3 tablespoons olive oil

1 medium onion, coarsely chopped

3 cloves garlic, crushed

2 pounds fresh tomatoes, coarsely chopped

$1/4$ teaspoon oregano

2 bay leaves

$1/2$ cup halved green olives

2 tablespoons capers

2 jalepeño chiles

Salt to taste

3 tablespoons olive oil

Preheat oven to 325 degrees. Place fillets in a lightly greased oval baking dish or rectangular Pyrex pan. Prick fillets on both sides with a fork. Massage with salt and lime juice.

In saucepan, sauté onions and garlic in 3 tablespoons oil until wilted but not brown. Add tomatoes and remaining ingredients, except for final 3 tablespoons olive oil. Cook over high heat about 10 minutes. Pour sauce over fish.

Sprinkle remaining oil over sauce and bake 20 minutes, uncovered. Turn fish over, and bake 10 more minutes. Baste frequently.

Excellent served with either white rice or hot tortillas. Also excellent served cold.

Serves 4–6

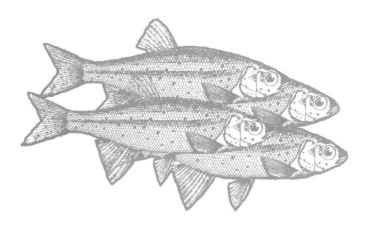

MEXICAN CORN BREAD

1 cup yellow cornmeal

¹/3 cup all-purpose flour

2 tablespoons sugar

1 teaspoon salt

2 teaspoons baking powder

¹/2 teaspoon baking soda

2 eggs, beaten

1 cup buttermilk

¹/2 cup vegetable oil

1 can (8³/4-oz.) cream-style corn

¹/3 cup chopped onion

2 tablespoons chopped green pepper

¹/2 cup shredded Cheddar cheese

Preheat oven to 350 degrees. In mixing bowl, combine first six ingredients. Combine remaining ingredients and add to dry ingredients. Stir only until moistened. Pour into greased 9-inch square baking pan or 10–inch heavy skillet. Bake 30–35 minutes or until bread is golden brown.   *Makes 12 squares or wedges*

JICAMA, CORN, AND MANGO SALAD

2 cans (7-oz. each) corn, drained

5 large mangoes, peeled, pitted, and roughly chopped

2 pounds jicama, peeled and chopped

1 cup chopped red onion

¹/2 cup chopped cilantro

¹/2 cup fresh lime juice

Put all ingredients in bowl. Season to taste with salt and pepper and toss to combine. Cover and chill.   *Serves 8–10*

YAM DULCE

1/2 cup sugar

1/4 cup water

2 pounds yams, cooked and mashed

1 teaspoon vanilla

1 teaspoon cinnamon

1 cup chopped pecans or walnuts

1/2 cup chopped, dried fruit of your choice
(We prefer apricots, candied pineapple,
and any of the candied citrus, orange,
lemon, or citron.)

2 ounces dark rum

Whipped cream or sour cream

Combine sugar and water in saucepan over very low heat, and stir to dissolve sugar. Turn heat to high and boil syrup until it reaches 225–230 degrees F. on a candy thermometer (thread stage). Add mashed yams to syrup and mix well. Stir in remaining ingredients except cream, and turn into shallow bowl.

Cover tightly with plastic wrap and chill in refrigerator for a minimum of three days. Top with whipped or sour cream and serve.

Serves 4–6

MRS. CHANG'S NOODLE SALAD

7 tablespoons dark sesame oil

7 tablespoons soy sauce

3 tablespoons balsamic vinegar

3–4 tablespoons sugar

2 1/2 teaspoons salt

1 tablespoon red pepper oil

8–10 scallions

3 tablespoons cilantro

1 pound spaghetti or angel hair pasta, cooked

Optional: snow pea pods

Optional: 2 cooked chicken breasts,
cut into bite-sized pieces (If you're
not also serving A Really Cute Chicken Dish.)

Whisk together first eight ingredients. Pour over pasta and stir. Add pea pods and/or chicken if desired. Chill.

Serves 6

A Really Cute Chicken Dish

8 cups chicken stock

4 thin slices fresh ginger

3 scallions coarsely chopped

One 4-pound chicken

GINGER SESAME SAUCE:

1 tablespoon fresh ginger, finely chopped

3 scallions, shredded

$^1/_2$ cup sugar

$^1/_4$ cup sesame oil

$^1/_4$ cup soy sauce

$^1/_2$ teaspoon hot red pepper flakes or to taste

Heat the first three ingredients. Place a metal spoon inside the chicken, and place chicken into the liquid. (This is the cute part in case you didn't catch it. The spoon retains the heat and allows the chicken to cook from the inside out and continue cooking when taken off the heat.) If the liquid does not completely cover the chicken, add boiling water to cover. Bring to boil and reduce heat to simmer. Cover and simmer 20 minutes.

Take pot off heat and leave chicken in broth for 2 hours. Remove and cut into large cubes (shish-kebob size).

SAUCE: Heat sauce ingredients in a small saucepan. Cool but do not chill. Dip chicken pieces into sauce or pour sauce over chicken.

Serves 4

PRESERVED KUMQUATS

1½ cups granulated sugar

1½ cups water

1 quart kumquats

Boil sugar and water 5 minutes. Cool. Meanwhile, wash kumquats; cut small cross in blossom end of each. Place in cooled syrup. Cover. Bring to a boil and simmer 1 hour or until clear. Do not remove cover at end of cooking time or fruit will shrink.

Remove covered saucepan from heat. Cool, with cover on, to room temperature. Pack in hot, sterilized jars. Cover with syrup and seal as jar manufacturer directs, or refrigerate for up to one week.

To serve in its simplest, lightest, and most authentic form, place 3 kumquats per person in small dessert bowls or wine glasses, with a few teaspoons of their own syrup in the bottom of each bowl. On other occasions, 1 or 2 kumquats make a lovely accompaniment to pound cake, vanilla ice cream, citrus or berry sherbets and sorbets, and to almond and other nut cookies.

Makes 4 cups fruit

After school, Billy the Bully's mother received multiple phone calls. Even though she was in the process of divorcing Billy's bigotted father, she still had to do something immediate to help her son shed ten years of paternal racist input.

WHAT Billy's mom served ...

BILLY'S CASSEROLE

3 cans (15-oz. each) pinto beans, drained

2 cans (15-oz. each) garbanzo beans, drained

1 cup white rice

3 cans (16-oz. each) stewed tomatoes

1 large onion, coarsely chopped

1 large green pepper, coarsely chopped

$^1/_2$ cup ketchup

$^1/_3$ cup honey

1 bunch mustard greens: washed thoroughly, drained and coarsely torn

1–2 pounds fully cooked brisket, cut into bite-sized pieces

1 tablespoon balsamic vinegar

Salt and pepper to taste

Preheat oven to 350 degrees. Put all ingredients except brisket, vinegar, and salt and pepper into large Dutch oven. Over medium heat bring mixture to a boil, stirring and dissolving honey.

Add brisket pieces. Cover and bake 30–40 minutes or until vegetables are tender and rice is cooked. Uncover and bake an additional 15 minutes. Season with balsamic vinegar and salt and pepper to taste.   *Serves 10*

LATER ...

When Billy's eyes lit up after his first scrumptious bite, his mom explained, "These are called garbanzo beans. They come from José's country. The long-grain rice that you love is Asian. Mrs. Robinson suggested the addition of the mustard greens, and Rachel's mom was kind enough to send over a few pieces of leftover brisket to flavor this remarkable dish. I think every ingredient is essential and holds its own. At the same time, they blend into a perfect taste sensation, so much greater than the sum of its parts. What do you think, William?"

11 Dinner Ad Nauseam
Meals You Can Make While Nauseated

You think that it's all in your womb, and then you find out your whole life is pregnant. —"Ourselves and Our Children," BOSTON WOMEN'S HEALTH BOOK COLLECTIVE

Kathy used to love surprises. Kathy, the Director of Development at the Madison, Wisconsin branch of Planned Parenthood, at the age of forty-five and with three teenagers ranging from thirteen to seventeen, thought she had a stomach virus. Surprise!

If she accurately recalled her past three pregnancies, this life-destroying, disgusting, clinical depression-inducing early morning sickness would pass in a mere seven months. In the meantime her family had to eat.

During pregnancy number three, she could hold her breath for as long as it took to whisk up some scrambled eggs and toast for two tiny toddler appetites.

During pregnancy number two, child number one ate only Cheerios. This simplified menu-planning for Kathy as she puked up her Saltines.

During pregnancy number one, she told her husband to get his own damned dinner.

But now she had three looming, lumbering monsters who each ate their own two-quart Corningware casserole of lasagna, a husband who came home for lunch, and a new brand of morning sickness which lasted well into dinner preparation hour and beyond. Frequent take-out was not feasible: Even if she was willing to let her loved ones eat horsemeat, dinner at Burger Hut for her current brood was a $75.00 tab.

WHAT TO SERVE?

Obviously, one woman's bland, safe food is another woman's barf-trigger.

Furthermore, the foods which stayed down during your first pregnancy may be the ones ruining your wardrobe during the second. Both of us found that working with ready-to-use chicken breasts somehow seemed less "triggering" than working with a whole dead chicken. Feel free to leave out any secondary ingredient which sickens you.

CHICKEN BREAST SAUTÉ WITH MUSHROOMS AND SCALLIONS

2 pounds skinless, boneless chicken breasts

Salt and pepper to taste

2 cloves garlic, minced

2 teaspoons oil of your choice

$^1/_4$ cup soy sauce

Juice of three limes

3 teaspoons fresh ginger, minced

2 tablespoons chopped scallions

8 ounces sliced shiitake mushrooms

Cut chicken breasts into thin strips. Sprinkle with salt and pepper. Sauté garlic in oil. Add chicken and sauté until white. Add soy sauce, lime juice, ginger, scallions, and mushrooms. Continue cooking until chicken is cooked through. Serve over rice. *Serves 4 hungry people*

Marinated Beef Kabobs

$1/2$ **cup bottled light Italian salad dressing**

$1/4$ **cup dry, red wine**

$1\,1/2$ **tablespoons soy sauce**

1 pound lean, boneless sirloin steak, cut into 1-inch cubes, excess fat removed

2 medium zucchini, cut into thick pieces

$1/2$ **medium red onion, cut into eighths**

8 fresh mushrooms

4 cherry tomatoes

Combine Italian dressing, wine, and soy sauce in shallow bowl. Place steak cubes in marinade and cover bowl. Refrigerate meat for at least 15 minutes (preferably several hours).

Steam zucchini for 3–4 minutes or until crisp-tender. Remove steak from marinade and reserve marinade for basting. Alternate steak and vegetables on skewers. Brush with marinade.

Grill 5 inches from coals, or broil on top rack for 10 minutes, brushing frequently with marinade. Serve with rice and salad.　*Serves 4*

Twice-Stuffed Potatoes for Really Queasy Days

Bake your favorite **large potatoes** in oven or microwave. Slice in half and scoop out potato pulp. Mash with **butter or olive oil, skim milk, salt, pepper,** and **Parmesan cheese**. You may add **chives, sour cream, chopped scallions, or bacon** to your liking. Alternatively, top with **Cheddar cheese**, and omit the Parmesan. Sprinkle with **paprika** and broil until crisp on top. For a light meal, simply serve with a green salad. For more substantial dining, serve with London Broil.

London Broil

Marinate lean **London Broil** in $1/2$ **cup red wine vinegar,** $1/2$ **cup soy sauce,** and **3 crushed garlic cloves**. Grill. This also works well with a butterflied turkey breast.

Basic Pregnancy Pasta Salad

¹/₂ pound unboringly shaped pasta, cooked

1 cup peas (fresh, or if frozen, defrosted)

¹/₂ cup diced sweet red pepper

¹/₂ cup diced red onion

1 cup fresh chopped basil (If you do not have fresh basil, do not used dried; substitute ¹/₂ cup chopped parsley.)

¹/₂ cup extra virgin olive oil

4 tablespoons fresh lime juice

Salt and pepper to taste

ADDITIONS:

1 pound cooked shrimp

¹/₂ pound sliced steak

1 pound grilled or steamed scallops

1 can (6-oz.) tuna

Combine pasta and vegetables. Whisk together oil, lime juice, salt, and pepper. Pour over salad and toss.

You have now made the Basic Pasta Salad, which, depending on your nausea level may remain basic. If your small intestine is feeling adventurous, add one or more of the additions.   *Serves 4*

Fast But Fancy Escarole and White Bean Soup

3 large heads escarole

2 tablespoons minced garlic

1 tablespoon olive oil

4 cans (14¹/₂-oz. each) of your favorite chicken broth

2 cans (14-oz. each) Great Northern beans, drained

Salt and pepper

Wash, drain, and chop escarole into large pieces. In large soup pot, sauté garlic in oil until brown. Add escarole and sauté until wilted. Add broth and beans. Salt and pepper to taste. Heat until boiling. Serve with a nourishing, whole grain bread.   *Serves 8*

KAREN WITH AN E'S EASY, HEALTHY CARROT SOUP

1 large onion, chopped

2 tablespoons butter

9 medium carrots, grated

1 large can (46-oz.) chicken broth

$1/8$ teaspoon white pepper

3 tablespoons raw white rice

1 tablespoon tomato paste

Parsley for garnish

In soup pot, sauté onion in butter. Add all remaining ingredients, except parsley, and cook until tender. Purée in batches in food processor until smooth, or use hand blender. Garnish with parsley.

Serves 8

BABY'S FIRST RICE PUDDING

1 cup Texmati or regular long grain rice (not converted)

4 cups skim milk

$1/2$ cup sugar

2 teaspoons vanilla

1 teaspoon ground cinnamon

$1/2$ teaspoon salt

$1/2$ cup raisins

Preheat oven to 325 degrees. In medium saucepan, combine rice, milk, sugar, vanilla, cinnamon, and salt. Heat to simmer. Simmer uncovered for 5 minutes. Add raisins and turn mixture into buttered, shallow 2-quart baking dish. Cover with foil. Bake until rice has absorbed most of the liquid, about 35–40 minutes. Remove from oven. Let stand 10 minutes before removing foil. Serve warm.

Makes 5 cups

FRESH PINEAPPLE WITH BERRY SAUCE

**1 package (10-oz.) frozen or 1 pint fresh
   raspberries**

^{1}/$_2$ cup sugar

1–2 tablespoons Kirsch

^{1}/$_2$ large pineapple

Fresh mint for garnish

Purée berries with their juice in a food mill or processor. Strain sauce to remove seeds. Stir sugar and Kirsch into purée. Sauce may be stored in refrigerator or frozen for up to three days.

    Cut pineapple into thin slices. Spoon some sauce onto each of four dessert plates. Place pineapple slices on top. Garnish with mint.

Serves 4

LATER ...

If this pregnancy had been planned, Kathy would not have suggested that her husband, Donald, complete his Master's Degree over five years of night school, thus excusing him from meal preparat ... okay, okay. No more B.S. Donald should be helping with the cooking. He isn't. And we all know that if Kathy were the one going to night school while working full-time and puking her Saltines, she would still have dinner on the table for her offspring. Thank goodness she at least tells Donald to get his own damned lunch.

12 The Invasion of Normandy
Entertaining Better Cooks Than You

Matrimony is a process by which a grocer acquired an account the florist had.
—Frances Rodman

Tom Smith is engaged to Bernadette-Genvieve St. Honore de Beaulieu. (Well, why not?)

They met three years ago when Tom spent his junior year in college living with the Beaulieus while he attended the Université de Normandy. Tom's fondest memories are of freshly baked baguettes each morning, the local *foie gras* for lunch, and dinners that ran the gamut from the sublime to the sublimer. And now the entire St. Honore de Beaulieu family was about to land at South Bend Indiana International Airport. They would be hungry.

Tom has been nagging his mother for the past month to enroll in a French cooking class, which she more than anyone would enjoy if she weren't holding down two jobs.

"Boeuf Bourguignon, Mom. Or at least Coq Au Vin, Spinach Soufflé, Potatoes Dauphine, and Endive with Raspberry Vinaigrette. And Napoleons because that's Mr. Beaulieu's specialty."

"Tom dear, speaking of things French, let me tell you a story about your Great Uncle Larry. During the war he was stationed near Giverny, and whenever he could, he would steal some serenity by visiting Monet's house and gardens. I know you went there, Tom, so you must remember how Monet had painted each room a different vibrant color. The kitchen was Wedgewood blue, the bedroom was a saturated pink, and the dining room was sunshine yellow. Uncle Larry loved it. Upon discharge, he went straight home and did the same thing to his house. Unfortunately, he lived in a semi-detached railroad flat in Detroit." Mrs. Smith waited for her son to ingest the lesson.

"Ah," said Tom after he had percolated twenty-five minutes.

What to serve?

Cheese in a Bread Bowl

Slice the top off of a **round sourdough bread**. Carefully scoop out most of the bread, leaving a $1/2$-inch thick bread bowl. Cut reserved bread pulp into cubes. Melt **Cheddar or Gruyère cheese** and pour into bread bowl. Use cubes of bread for dipping.

Pigs in Blankets

Purchase **packaged crescent roll dough**. Separate into triangles. Roll a **cocktail hot dog** into each triangle. Brush with **beaten egg**. Bake at 350 degrees until dough is brown and flaky and hot dogs are cooked.

Makes 8 pigs in blankets per crescent roll package

SPECIAL PEA PODS AND RADISHES

$^3/_4$ **pound sugar snap peas, trimmed**

$^1/_2$ **cup water**

1 tablespoon unsalted butter

1 bunch radishes, very thinly sliced

Salt and pepper

$^1/_4$ **teaspoon chopped tarragon**

Cook peas in boiling water for 1 minute. Pour off water and add butter, radishes, salt, pepper, and tarragon. Toss well.   *Serves 6*

BRUSSELS SPROUTS AMERICANA

2 pounds Brussels sprouts

4 tablespoons butter

$^1/_4$ **cup granulated brown sugar**

2 tablespoons honey mustard

1 teaspoon white horseradish

Pepper

Steam Brussels sprouts until tender. Whisk together remaining ingredients and heat until warm. Pour over Brussels sprouts. Serve hot or at room temperature.   *Serves 6*

GRILLED BARBECUED PORTABELLO MUSHROOMS

Brush **portabello mushrooms** with **barbecue sauce** and grill. Serve on **hamburger buns** with **tomato** and **onion**, if desired.

CORN ON THE COB

Husk it. Boil it. Butter it. Salt it. Eat it.

Pumpkin Raisin Bread

1 cup corn oil

4 eggs, beaten

$^2/_3$ cup water

2 cups canned pumpkin

3$^1/_3$ cups sifted flour

1$^1/_2$ teaspoons salt

1 teaspoon nutmeg

1 teaspoon cinnamon

2 teaspoons baking soda

2 cups sugar

1 cup raisins

1$^1/_4$ cups chopped pecans

Preheat oven to 350 degrees. Grease and flour two 9 x 5 x 3-inch loaf pans. Mix oil, eggs, water, and pumpkin. Add flour, salt, nutmeg, cinnamon, baking soda, and sugar. Mix in raisins and nuts. Bake 1 hour.   *Makes 2 loaves*

Roast Turkey

Wash **turkey** thoroughly with hot water. Pluck any remaining feathers. Put turkey into a disposable roasting pan. Sprinkle with **garlic salt, paprika,** and **rosemary**. For extra crispy skin, sprinkle lightly with **flour**. Tent with heavy-duty foil. Bake at 500 degrees 15 minutes. Reduce heat to 375 degrees and roast 13 minutes per pound until done. At 45 minutes before the turkey is finished, remove foil, baste, and return to oven for final roasting.

Cherry-Cranberry Compote

2 cans (16-oz. each) **whole cranberry sauce**

1 can (28-oz.) **pitted Bing cherries**

1 tablespoon **grated orange peel**

$^1/_2$ cup **toasted walnuts**

Heat all ingredients except nuts until sauce melts. Stir in nuts. Chill.   *Serves 6*

Fresh Tuna Burgers With Piquant Asian Glaze

GLAZE:

$^1/_3$ **cup tamari sauce**

2 teaspoons minced ginger

$^1/_2$ **teaspoon minced garlic**

1 tablespoon honey

1 tablespoon Dijon mustard

$^1/_2$ **teaspoon rice vinegar**

BURGERS:

$1^1/_2$ **pounds fresh ground tuna. Remove all gristle and skin.**

1 shallot, minced

3 tablespoons Dijon mustard

3 drops Tabasco Sauce

Salt and pepper

Hamburger buns

Combine all Glaze ingredients in small saucepan and bring to boil. Lower heat and simmer for 3 minutes. Strain and reserve.

(If your fish market will not grind the tuna for you, grind it yourself in a meat grinder, or chop it with a sharp knife until it resembles hamburger meat.)

For Burgers, combine tuna with shallot, mustard, Tabasco, salt, and pepper. Form into patties. Grill. Serve on buns, with a spoonful of Glaze. *Serves 6–8 depending on how large you like your burgers*

APPLE FRENCH TOAST

1 cup packed brown sugar

1 stick butter or margarine

2 tablespoons light corn syrup

2 large tart apples, peeled and sliced
$^1/_4$-inch thick

3 eggs

1 cup milk

1 teaspoon vanilla

9 slices day-old French bread

SYRUP:

1 cup applesauce

1 jar (10-oz.) apple butter

$^1/_2$ teaspoon cinnamon

$^1/_8$ teaspoon ground cloves

Preheat oven to 350 degrees. In small saucepan, cook brown sugar, butter, and syrup until thick, about 5–7 minutes. Pour into ungreased 13 x 9 x 2-inch baking pan. Arrange apples on top. In a mixing bowl, beat eggs, milk, and vanilla. Dip bread slices into egg mixture for 1 minute. Place soaked bread over apples. Cover and refrigerate overnight. Remove from refrigerator 30 minutes before baking.

Bake, uncovered, for 35–40 minutes.

SYRUP: Combine ingredients in medium saucepan. Cook and stir until hot. Serve over French toast. *Serves 9*

APPLE CRISP PIZZA

PIZZA:

1 frozen pastry shell, partially defrosted

$^2/_3$ cup sugar

3 tablespoons all-purpose flour

1 teaspoon cinnamon

4 medium baking apples, peeled and cut into $^1/_2$-inch slices

TOPPING:

$^1/_2$ cup all-purpose flour

$^1/_3$ cup packed brown sugar

$^1/_3$ cup rolled oats

1 teaspoon cinnamon

4 tablespoons butter or margarine

$^1/_4$ to $^1/_2$ cup caramel ice cream topping or caramel apple dip

Optional: **vanilla ice cream**

Preheat oven to 350 degrees. Roll pastry shell to fit a 12-inch pizza pan. Fold under or flute the edges. Combine sugar, flour, and cinnamon in a bowl. Add apples and toss. Arrange apples in single layer in a circular pattern to completely cover pastry.

TOPPING: Combine first five Topping ingredients. Sprinkle over apples. Bake pizza for 35–40 minutes or until apples are tender. Remove from oven and immediately drizzle with caramel topping or dip. Serve warm with ice cream, if desired. *Serves 8–10*

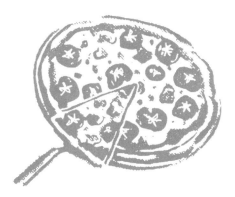

THREE CHOCOLATE FUDGE

3^1/3 cups sugar

2 sticks butter or margarine

1 cup packed dark brown sugar

1 can (12-oz.) evaporated milk

32 large marshmallows, halved

2 cups (12 ounces) semisweet
chocolate chips

2 milk chocolate candy bars
(7-oz. each), broken

2 squares (1-oz. each) semisweet
baking chocolate, chopped

1 teaspoon vanilla

2 cups chopped walnuts

In large saucepan, combine first four ingredients. Cook and stir over medium heat until sugar is dissolved. Bring to rapid boil and let boil 5 minutes, stirring constantly. Remove from heat. Stir in marshmallows until melted. Stir in chocolate chips until melted. Add chocolate bars and baking chocolate and stir until melted. Fold in vanilla and walnuts. Mix well. Pour into greased 15 x 10 x 1-inch baking pan. Chill until firm. Cut into squares.   *Serves 10–12*

LATER ...

Mom and Tom could not satiate the Beaulieus' appetite for Tollhouse Cookies (see package for recipe). Indeed, a year later the wedding was a model of transatlantic synergy. Crêpes Escargots sat beside Pigs in Blankets, and each lucky guest was sent home with a slice of Gâteau Fourré à la Crème d'Orange and a Rice Krispie Square (see box for recipe).

13 The Jack Sprat Dilemma
When He's on Atkins and You're on Ornish
(The Compromise Diet)

The great companies did not know that the line between hunger and anger is a thin one. —John Steinbeck

Glen was 6'3" but weighed only 168 pounds. Cynthia was 5'6" and weighed, sopping wet, 121 pounds. Naturally, they both decided to go on a diet.

Glen was born with a death wish, so he chose one of the very popular unlimited fat and protein/zero carbohydrate diets. Cynthia, born extremist, chose to eliminate all fat, red meat, sugar, white flour, and taste from her life. Consequently, each followed their own guru-doctor. Glen practically lived on Dr. Filbert's Cream of Cream Soup with a side of Saddle of Lamb. His wife watched him enviously, as she crunched without surcease on Dr. Green's Hearty Cucumber Stew with a dessert of blanched enoki mushroom sorbet.

Given that Cynthia's health history was so flawless that radical changes could only jeopardize it, and given that Glen's Christmas gift to his parents were His-and-Hers Quintuple Bypasses, they began to rethink. Also, the time required for formulating shopping lists and food preparation precluded them from making babies. Which they wanted. They thought. Also, they were viciously tempted by each other's plates. They couldn't go on like this.

Perhaps the answer lay in moderation … and in the first lifestyle compromise of Cynthia's and Glen's marriage.

What to serve?

Lebnah and Accessories

Lebnah is Middle Eastern yogurt cheese, and indispensable to fat-phobic cuisine. It substitutes for sour cream, mayonnaise, crème fraîche, and the more caloric and fattier cheeses and dips. Here's how to make and serve it for an appetizer, brunch, or light luncheon. There are fancy lebnah gadgets out there, but who has the time to unearth one in Actual Real Life?

Classic Lebnah

4 cups plain yogurt (regular and low-fat are fine, but the nonfat won't work)

Before going to bed, put a mesh strainer over a bowl—make sure the bottom of the strainer is a good few inches above the bottom of the bowl.

Everyone advises lining the strainer with 4 layers of cheesecloth, so do that if you possess cheesecloth. We use our husbands' worn (laundered) hankies and wake up to lebnah just the same.

Dump the yogurt into the lined strainer. Fold the residual cheesecloth or handkerchief over the top; if there's not enough fabric for this, simply top with a plate. Refrigerate overnight, or at least 8 hours.   *Makes approximately 3 cups Lebnah*

CHAYA'S LEBNAH

The unadorned, classic way to serve lebnah is very lightly drizzled with olive oil. But the following version makes Cynthia and Glen feel like they're vacationing somewhere trendy in Eilat.

1^1/2 **teaspoons lightly toasted sesame seeds**

^{1}/2 **teaspoon salt**

^{1}/4 **teaspoon crushed green peppercorns**

^{1}/4 **teaspoon zatar* or dried marjoram**

^{1}/8 **teaspoon ground cumin**

1 **recipe Classic Lebnah (see above)**

1 **tablespoon of the best olive oil you can afford**

Mix everything except lebnah and olive oil in a small bowl. Lift the yogurt cheese lebnah in the cheesecloth from strainer and carefully turn out onto a round platter. Drizzle with olive oil. Sprinkle with sesame seed mixture (patting it a bit so it stays put and pretty).

For hors d'oeuvres, brunch, or lunch, accompany either version of lebnah with fat-free bagel chips, pita chips, or whole wheat pita wedges, brine-cured olives, and colorful raw vegetables. For breakfast, substitute it for cream cheese on your bagel, English muffin, or bran muffin.

Makes 3 cups

*Zatar is an herb available dried at Middle Eastern groceries, but marjoram is almost as authentic.

Med-Med* Soup

Just your usual Tuscan tofu combo, this fragrant soup is an aggressively wholesome first course, all-in-one dinner with a great bread, or a convenient and reviving thermos lunch.

2 tablespoons olive oil

1 cup chopped leeks (white part only)

$^1/_3$ cup diced fennel (from the stalk or bulb—save the feathery tips for garnish)

3 garlic cloves, minced

$^1/_2$ teaspoon dried basil

$^1/_2$ teaspoon dried thyme

3 cups defatted chicken stock, water, or vegetable stock

1 pound firm tofu, cut into 1-inch cubes (forget pressing)

3 cups chopped fresh tomatoes (forget skinning or seeding) or the same amount of undrained canned tomatoes

$^1/_8$ teaspoon saffron (no more no matter how affluent you are!)

1 cup cooked brown rice

Salt and pepper to taste

In nonstick pan, heat olive oil and sauté leeks, fennel, garlic, basil, and thyme for 5 minutes. Add stock or water, tofu, and tomatoes. Simmer gently for 15-20 minutes. Add saffron and brown rice, salt and pepper to taste. Simmer another minute or two. *Serves 4–6*

*Medicinal-Mediterranean

SPICY ALMOST-ASIAN SALAD

^{1}/2 cup *each*: **green peppers, carrot, daikon radish, red onion, and cucumber—all thinly sliced**

1 cup alfalfa sprouts

1 bunch of carefully washed and dried spinach

3 tablespoons *each*: lemon juice, white vinegar, and Thai fish sauce (for vegetarians, substitute tamari or mirin)

Toss all ingredients together.   *Serves 6*

Baked Sea Bass with Balsamic Onions on Whole Wheat Couscous

THE FISH:

Vegetable oil spray

4 to 6 one-third pound pieces of sea bass fillets

1 large lemon, juiced

Salt and pepper

THE ONIONS:

2 tablespoons olive oil

3 hefty onions (red, Vidalia, yellow, or a mixture) cut into sixteenths

$1/2$ cup balsamic vinegar

2 tablespoons honey (one of the darker varieties is best)

Pinch of cayenne pepper

THE COUSCOUS:

$2 2/3$ cups water

1 teaspoon salt

2 cups whole wheat couscous

Optional garnish: **Oven-Dried Tomatoes and flat leaf parsley**

Preheat oven to 450 degrees. Spray baking sheet, then place fish on it. Douse each fillet in fresh lemon juice. Sprinkle with salt and pepper. Bake 10 minutes.

Reduce heat to 225 degrees with rack in middle of oven. Line a baking sheet with parchment paper. In skillet, sauté the small onion wedges in olive oil over medium-high heat. To get them brown enough takes a good 7 minutes; keep stirring. Add balsamic vinegar, honey, and cayenne, and continue stirring over medium heat for 1 more minute.

Spread onions in one even layer on parchment-lined sheet. Bake $1 1/4$ hours, or until onions are a bit crispy and most of the syrup has been absorbed. Cool in bowl.

May be made 1 day ahead, stored airtight and refrigerated. Bring to room temperature or warm slightly when ready to serve. These onions are extremely dark and intense, and pack a ton of flavor into almost no fat.

For the couscous, bring water and salt to boil. Stir in couscous, cover, turn off heat, and let stand 10 minutes. Fluff with fork. (When not adding olive oil or butter to couscous, make right before serving.)

ASSEMBLY:

On each plate make a bed of couscous. Top with a piece of fish. Then drape the onions with great spontaneity over both couscous and fish. If you like, garnish with Oven-Dried Tomatoes (see page 171) and big bouquets of flat leaf parsley.

Serves 4

TRIPLE ORANGE LONDON BROIL

Evolved eating does not mean never having red meat. Careful removal of fat and portion control via paper-thin slices turn a hearty he-man favorite into a gastro-politically-correct treat.

2 tablespoons cornstarch

1 cup fresh orange juice (Save 2 teaspoons of this for final step, and, if garnishing, zest the orange peel and reserve.)

1 large onion, thinly sliced

4 cloves garlic, minced

2 tablespoons soy or tamari sauce (low-sodium is fine)

$^{3}/_{4}$ teaspoon fresh ginger, grated

$^{1}/_{4}$–$^{1}/_{2}$ teaspoon red pepper flakes to taste

1 tablespoon brown sugar

$^{3}/_{4}$ pound London Broil, very thinly sliced and cut into 3-inch lengths *(Partially freeze the raw steak to facilitate slicing.)*

1 cup snow peas

1 cup fresh asparagus spears, cut in thirds (after removing tough end)

Optional: **$^{1}/_{2}$ cup water chestnuts, sliced**

1 cup fresh orange wedges, halved, or 1 cup canned mandarin orange slices, drained

Steamed white or brown rice

Optional garnish: **orange zest and red radish spirals**

Dissolve cornstarch in reserved 2 teaspoons orange juice and $^{1}/_{2}$ cup cold water. Whisk thoroughly.

Prepare a marinade of orange juice, onion, garlic, soy sauce, ginger, red pepper flakes, and brown sugar. Immerse beef slices for 1 hour to overnight. Lightly spray or oil a wok (or use a large, nonstick skillet). Stir-fry beef and onions (reserved from marinade) 3–5 minutes over medium-high heat. Add snow peas, asparagus, and optional water chestnuts; cover pan and let cook for 2 more minutes. Add orange wedges and combine gently.

Pushing the solids to the side of your wok or skillet, add the cornstarch mixture to the pan liquid, whisk 1 minute, then very gently stir thickened liquid and solids together. Serve over steamed rice.

This bright dish demands no garnish, but if you wish, top with orange zest and red radish spirals. Truly a one-dish meal, you don't even need a salad, but fresh fruit for dessert or K'leen's Sorbet would be perfect.   *Serves 4*

K'leen's Sorbet

Fat-free, work-free, low in calories, and icily refreshing, this sorbet (and you) earn the bit of sugar inherent to good canned fruit. The recipe does not work with the "lite" stuff.

1 large can (29-oz.) any fruit in heavy syrup (Use any and all kinds: pears, plums, peaches, etc.)

2 tablespoons juice from any citrus fruit or a liqueur (Kirsch, Cointreau, peach brandy, etc.)

Freeze fruit in unopened can for 4–8 hours. Dip in hot water to free from can. Chop with a fork, then put in processor with the citrus juice or liqueur. Process to sherbert consistency and serve immediately. Fitting as is for the diet-conscious menu (or as a mid-meal palate cleanser!), this recipe is delightful for impurer occasions when served in sugar cones or waffle bowls.   *Serves 6*

Later ...

While legitimately overweight people almost always lose weight on this type of program, after three months of strict adherence neither Cynthia nor Glen lost more than a few ounces. They began the journey to self-acceptance, while appreciating the positive changes in their cholesterol, triglyceride, and lipid levels. Not to mention the scads of energy, which led to the creation of Baby Molly on the night of their only cheat: eating cheesecake off each other's washboard abs.

14 Jack Sprat Dilemma II
When He's on Atkins and You're on Ornish
(The Each Person for Him/Herself Diet)

We are our choices. —Jean-Paul Sartre

Okay, okay. Our original chapter title promised you a solution to the dilemma of preparing meals when one's household's diets are extremely divergent. And here it is: Layer cooking.

Layer cooking is like layer dressing. You prepare the components as you would for any unrestricted meal. But assembly is left to the individual dieter, not the cook. Example: The Doe family prepares two roast chickens, baked potatoes, salad, vinaigrette, steamed broccoli, and apple crisp. Jane, who is on the Ornish low-fat program, takes a piece of the white meat, removes the skin, eats half a potato (with one tablespoon of fat-free sour cream), a generous portion of broccoli, and squeezes lemon wedges on her salad. She skips the crisp.

John, who is religious in his adherence to the Atkins diet, eats almost an entire chicken with the skin, pours butter over a moderate portion of broccoli, and slathers his salad in vinaigrette. He skips the potatoes and the crisp.

Jane Junior, the only Doe comfortable with moderation, eats a moderate portion of everything.

John Junior is late for his basketball game. He grabs an oozing handful of apple crisp on his way out. (Yes, we know this is nutritionally unsound. But remember ... Actual Real Life?)

Grandma Doe eats a Godzilla portion of everything, with seconds on the crisp. She is rather mystified by these new-fangled eating regimes. She is 102 years old.

15 Peace of Cake
What to Serve After a Falling Out

Men become what they are, sons of God, by becoming what they are, brothers of their brothers. —Martin Buber

Stu and Len owned a large chain of appliance stores which, with the fertile imagination stereotypically attributed to appliance salesmen, they named Stu and Len's Appliances.

The Overbrook Park, Kansas store was failing. Didn't anybody in the Bread Basket of the Nation need bread machines or ovens or mixers or refrigerators? Len said, "Sell the rotten place. It's bleeding us dry."

Stu replied, "If we had sold the Detroit store when you wanted to, you wouldn't be folding your fat butt into that low-slung BMW you drive."

Len. "My fat butt has nothing on your fat head. We're losing money, you idiot! Stubborn! That's what you've always been, and look what it did to us on the Philadelphia deal."

Stu. "Whoa. That's below the belt. You promised you'd never mention Philly."

Len. "I'll tell you what I'll mention. I'll mention letting your lazy bum of a kid 'work' New Orleans last summer. How could anyone not sell one lousy air conditioner in New Orleans in the summer?"

Stu. "Talk about my son, huh? Well, if anything's fair game, hows about we talk about your wife ... "

That evening, Stu and Len went home and told their wives about the falling-out. "Here we go again," said Anastasia and Lynette, "your house or mine?"

WHAT TO SERVE?

ARUGULA-RADICCHIO-FENNEL SALAD

7 tablespoons olive oil

3 tablespoons fresh lemon juice

3 shallots, minced

2 small, fresh fennel bulbs, trimmed and cut vertically into thin slices

4$^1/_2$ cups bite-size pieces radicchio

2 bunches arugula, cut into bite-size pieces

Garnish: 6 sliced, pitted black olives

Whisk olive oil, lemon juice, and minced shallot in small bowl. Season with salt and pepper.

Toss fennel, radicchio, and arugula with dressing in medium bowl. Divide between six plates and garnish with olives.   *Serves 6*

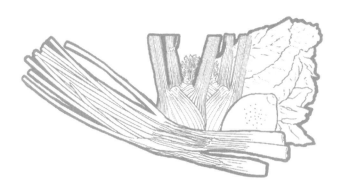

Roasted Peppers, Eggplant, and Mozzarella Salad

6 ripe, red peppers

2 medium eggplants

Olive oil to coat

$1/2$ pound fresh Mozzarella cheese, sliced

3 tablespoons capers

DRESSING:

3 tablespoons olive oil

6 tablespoons balsamic vinegar

1 tablespoon Dijon mustard

Juice of $1/2$ lemon

Line a broiler pan tray with foil. Place red peppers on tray and place tray under broiler. Broil until skin is charred and black. Turn peppers and continue broiling until entire pepper is black. Remove from oven and place peppers in a paper bag. Fold bag shut and let stand five minutes.

While waiting for peppers, peel and slice eggplant into $1/2$-inch slices. Brush each slice with olive oil, place on the foil-lined broiler tray and broil until starting to brown. Turn slices, brush with oil, and broil until eggplant slices are tender. Remove from oven.

Cut stems off red peppers and slice in half lengthwise. Seed peppers and remove charred, outer skin.

On each of six plates, overlap slices of pepper, Mozzarella, and eggplant. Sprinkle capers over each plate.

DRESSING: Whisk together olive oil, balsamic vinegar, mustard, and lemon juice. Drizzle over salad.   *Serves 6*

PEAR, WALNUT, AND CURLY ENDIVE SALAD

6 teaspoons sherry wine vinegar

3 teaspoons Dijon mustard

7 tablespoons olive oil

$^3/_4$ teaspoon dried thyme, crumbled

Salt and pepper

9 cups bite-size pieces curly endive (about one large head)

3 large, ripe pears, cut into quarters, cored, and sliced crosswise

$^3/_4$ cup chopped walnuts

Combine vinegar and mustard in small bowl. Gradually whisk in oil. Mix in thyme. Season with salt and pepper.

Combine endive and pear in large bowl. Add dressing and toss to coat. Divide among six plates. Sprinkle with walnuts.   *Serves 6*

MARILYN'S CHICKEN FRICASSÉE

WINGS:

3 onions, chopped

3 tablespoons canola oil

$^1/_2$ teaspoon salt

$^1/_8$ teaspoon pepper

$^1/_8$ teaspoon paprika

2 pounds chicken wings

MEATBALLS:

1$^1/_2$ pounds lean ground sirloin

1$^1/_2$ pounds ground turkey

2 eggs

2 tablespoons bread crumbs

Salt and pepper to taste

Water equivalent to the eggs (Fill half of an eggshell with water 4 times.)

In a large saucepan or Dutch oven, sauté onions in canola oil over medium heat until golden brown. Season with salt, pepper, and paprika. Add chicken wings and sear on all sides. Allow onions to stick to bottom of pot as wings are searing. Scrape pot frequently. When wings are seared on all sides, add cold water to cover. Set aside while you make meatballs.

MEATBALLS: Combine all ingredients and form into meatballs about 1$^1/_2$ inches in circumference. Bring salted water to a boil and add meatballs. Boil for 5 minutes. When meatballs have cooked, drain and place in Dutch oven with wings. Cook on low simmer 1 hour. Serve with rice, couscous, or kasha.

Serves 8–10

CHICKEN WITH BRANDIED PLUM SAUCE

CHICKEN:
  4 whole, boneless chicken breasts, split
  Salt and pepper

SAUCE:
  2 cans (14-oz. each) purple plums
  1 scant cup sherry
  2 tablespoons cornstarch
  1/4 cup orange juice
  2/3 cup Grand Marnier, divided in half

Preheat oven to 300 degrees. Salt and pepper breasts. Place breasts in a baking pan and cover with foil. Bake 1 hour. Uncover chicken and place breasts on broiler pan. Broil just until brown.

SAUCE: While chicken is in its last half-hour of cooking time, prepare sauce. Strain plums, retaining juice in a bowl. Mix juice with sherry. Bring to boiling over medium heat. Cool. Dissolve cornstarch in orange juice and slowly add to sherry mixture. Simmer 15–20 minutes stirring frequently until desired thickness is reached. Remove from heat. Adjust flavor with orange juice and/or sherry. Heat 1/3 cup Grand Marnier in separate saucepan. Add it to the sauce and flambé. Add the plums and heat through.

ASSEMBLY: Keeping the bulk of the sauce in its saucepan, steal enough of it to brush the chicken in order to keep it thoroughly moist; leave baking pan in oven with heat off until ready to serve.

When ready to serve, separately heat the remaining 1/3 cup Grand Marnier. At tableside, pour it into the plum sauce and flambé. When flames have thoroughly died, spoon sauce over chicken. *Serves 8*

LAMB SHANKS WITH PORCINI, WHITE BEANS, AND FARFALLE

1 ounce dried porcini mushrooms

1 cup hot water

3^1/2 tablespoons olive oil

6 lamb shanks (about ^{3}/4 pound each)

All-purpose flour

1 large onion, chopped

2 fresh rosemary sprigs or 1 teaspoon dried, chopped rosemary

2 bay leaves

1 can (28-oz.) Italian plum tomatoes, with liquid

1^1/2 cups chicken stock

1 cup dry white wine

2 cans (15-oz. each) Great Northern beans, drained

^{3}/4 pound farfalle (bow-tie pasta)

1 cup freshly grated Parmesan cheese

Chopped, fresh rosemary

Place mushrooms in bowl. Cover with hot water and let stand until softened, about 30 minutes. Drain mushrooms, reserving soaking liquid. Coarsely chop mushrooms.

Heat 2 tablespoons olive oil in large stockpot or Dutch oven over medium-high heat. Dredge lamb shanks in flour and shake off excess. Add to pot, sprinkle with salt and pepper, and brown well on all sides. Transfer to plate. Add chopped onion, rosemary sprigs, and bay leaves, and sauté until onion is tender, about 7 minutes. Add mushrooms with their soaking liquid, canned tomatoes with their juices, chicken stock, and wine. Break up tomatoes with spoon. Return lamb to pan, spooning tomatoes and liquid over it. Reduce heat, cover, and simmer 1^1/2 hours. (Lamb may be prepared 1 day ahead. Refrigerate covered.)

Add beans to lamb mixture. Season to taste with salt and pepper. Cook uncovered until lamb is very tender and cooking liquid thickens slightly, stirring frequently, about 45 minutes. Spoon off fat from surface.

Cook pasta in large pot of rapidly boiling salted water until tender, but still firm. Drain well. Return to pot. Add remaining olive oil and toss thoroughly to coat.

Divide pasta between 6 plates. Top each with 1 lamb shank. Spoon sauce over. Sprinkle with Parmesan cheese and chopped rosemary.

Serves 6

Jackie's "I Forgot What I Was Mad About" Chocolate Cake

1 package extra moist German chocolate cake mix

1 can (14-oz.) Eagle Brand sweetened condensed milk

³/₄ jar of Mrs. Richardson's caramel butterscotch fudge sauce

Optional: **5–6 Heath candy bars or 10–12 Oreo cookies or 2 Snickers candy bars, crushed**

1 cup whipping cream

¹/₂ cup sugar

1 teaspoon vanilla

Prepare cake mix as directed on package using a 9 x 13 x 2-inch pan. When cake is cooled, poke holes all over the top of the cake with the handle of a wooden spoon. Holes should be slightly smaller than the size of a dime. Pour condensed milk over the cake letting it seep into the holes. Wait five minutes and pour the caramel butterscotch fudge over the cake. Refrigerate for several hours.

If desired, sprinkle crushed Heath bars or Oreo cookies or Snickers Bars over the cake. Whip the cream with the sugar and vanilla until peaks form. Serve with the cake.   *Serves 15*

POACHED PEARS IN CHOCOLATE SABAYON

This light, chocolate sauce does not overwhelm the delicate flavor of pears.

6 ripe Comice or Bosc pears

3 cups water

1 cup sugar

1 piece lemon rind

1 stick cinnamon (2 inches)

4 ounces semisweet chocolate

³/₄ cup coffee

6 egg yolks

5 tablespoons sugar

¹/₄ cup pear brandy or cognac, divided

Optional: **1 cup whipping cream and 2 tablespoons confectioners' sugar**

Peel whole pears leaving stem intact. In large saucepan big enough to hold pears, combine water, 1 cup sugar, lemon rind, and cinnamon. Heat to boiling. Add pears. Cover and poach until tender. Let pears cool in pan syrup. Refrigerate overnight.

Melt chocolate in ¹/₄ cup coffee. In a double boiler, mix yolks and 5 tablespoons sugar. Add melted chocolate and remaining coffee. Stir mixture over simmering water until creamy and thickened. Add 2 tablespoons brandy.

Whip cream. Add sugar and 2 tablespoons brandy. Place a pear on each of 6 dessert plates. Drizzle with sauce and top with a dollop of whipped cream, if desired.   *Serves 6*

CARROT PINEAPPLE CAKE

CAKE:

4 eggs

2 cups sugar

1¹/₂ cups oil

2 cups sifted flour

2 teaspoons cinnamon

2 teaspoons soda

¹/₂ teaspoon salt

3 cups grated carrots

1 can (8-oz.) crushed pineapple, drained

¹/₂ cup chopped nuts

ICING:

1 stick butter or margarine

1 pound confectioners' sugar

1 package (8-oz.) cream cheese

2 teaspoons vanilla

Preheat oven to 350 degrees. Beat eggs well. Add sugar and oil. Sift together flour, cinnamon, soda, and salt. Blend into egg mixture. Fold in carrots, pineapple, and nuts. Pour batter into a greased 9 x 13 x 2-inch pan and bake 50–60 minutes. Cool.

ICING: Combine ingredients and beat until smooth. Spread on cooled cake.   *Serves 15*

LATER ...

Yeah, this sounds sexist. We made the guys the professionals and stuck the female characters in the kitchen, patching up relationships free-of-charge. But the reality is, if Anastasia and Lynette had spent every waking moment of the past fifteen years building an appliance empire, they probably wouldn't know how to cook either.

• •

16 Preventing Mom's Suicide
PMS Food

No issue is so small that it can't be blown out of proportion. —Stuart Hughes

Screw this chapter! Who wants to write a freakin' cookbook anyway? Who the hell needs another cookbook? Who the hell do we think we are—the frickin' Brontë sisters? Sure they could write! Neither one of them had husbands or children! And where did these fruggin' three pounds come from? We've been foogin' starving ourselves! Where the fulk is that fulkin' chocolate bar? Who the hell cares if we ever look good again?

Laura: "Karin! Where are the floppy discs? You said you bought floppy discs! How could you not buy floppy discs? (crying) This whole manuscript is going to end up ... disappeared. I just know it!"

Karin: "I freegin' forgot ... OKAY?"

WHAT TO SERVE?

THE BAD GIRL MENU

Best friends often find themselves on the same cycle, so make sure to have plenty to share.

Instructional note: There are four basic PMS food groups.

Sweet	**Crunchy**
Salty	**Creamy**

It is vital to have a balanced selection from the above four categories within five days after ovulation. This month our meal of choice included a Chocolate Caramel Marshmallow Reese's Pieces Bananaless Split with Real Whipped Cream and Cool Whip with a Garnish of Potato Chips.

Bad Girl Later ...

Laura: "What a hoot! Sixteen chapters floating around in the cyberkitchen never to be found! Wow, Kar! What's that, three months work down the drain?"

Karin: (laughing) "Frees me up to work on Andrew's Bar Mitzvah. I remembered to get everything for the Bar Mitzvah except the place. Ha, ha, ha. Every place I've called within a forty-mile radius is booked! Could you die?"

Laura: "What a hoot! And guess what else? Sibyl Publications is having second thoughts about publishing us. They say we're acting unprofessional. Ha, ha, ha, ha, ha, ha, ha, ha, ha."

Karin: "More ice cream?"

Laura: "Yes. And make it à la mode."

THE GOOD GIRL MENU

Here is the prevailing wisdom regarding PMS and diet. It's not fun. And it's also probably not news to you. Experts strongly suggest that we afflicted ones be extra vigilant in our nutrition regime during the week prior to menstruation. Studies suggest that during this part of the cycle, our livers and kidneys are working hard to metabolize excess estrogen and other hormone metabolites, so don't give them additional work to do. Avoid processed foods as much as possible. Sodas with their heavy phosphate load are *verboten*. Cut back significantly on caffeine (no more than two cups of coffee daily, less if you can function without). And while you're cutting back, don't forget about fat. High levels of fat in the diet can increase anxiety, and cause food cravings.

Help yourself to plenty of fresh fruits and vegetables. A little chocolate can actually make us feel better, so learn to set limits and enjoy a bite or two.

We realize this is a cookbook and not a holistic health manual, but it is important to include dietary supplements in this chapter. PMS symptoms can be significantly relieved by popping the following capsules:

Vitamin B-6: 50–150 mg. daily

Evening Primrose Oil: 500 mg. 2–4 times daily

Calcium: 1000 mg. daily

Don't forget to exercise! Endorphins can blunt the highs and lows of premenstrual stress days. Learn to like your body instead of being angry at it all the time.

All the recipes in chapter 2. Call Me Indigestible are suitable for PMS as well.

BABY GREENS AND WHITE BEAN SALAD

1^1/2 tablespoons balsamic vinegar

^{1}/2 tablespoon olive oil

1 tablespoon orange juice

2 teaspoons Dijon mustard

1 clove garlic, minced

^{1}/4 teaspoon sugar

^{1}/4 teaspoon pepper

6 cups mixed baby greens (mesclun)

1 can (15-oz.) cannellini or Great
   Northern beans

^{1}/2 cup roasted red pepper strips

8 canned artichoke hearts, halved

Optional: purchased croutons

For the dressing, whisk together vinegar, oil, orange juice, mustard, garlic, sugar, and pepper.

Combine greens, beans, pepper strips, and artichoke hearts in large bowl. Toss with dressing. Top with croutons, if desired.

Makes 4 side dish servings

CITRUS FRUIT COMPOTE

1 lemon

2 clementines (cross between a
   tangerine and an orange)

1 lime

2 tablespoons sugar

2 large pears, cored and sliced

2 medium mangoes, peeled and cubed

1 cup seedless red grapes

Halve the lemon, clementines, and lime, saving the rinds. Squeeze out all juices. (You should have about ^{3}/4 cup.) Combine citrus juice and sugar in a small saucepan. Add half the citrus rinds. Bring to boil, stirring until sugar is dissolved. Reduce heat and simmer, uncovered 5 minutes. Discard rinds.

Combine pears, mangoes, and grapes in large bowl. Pour hot syrup over fruit, gently stirring to mix. Cover and chill for up to 4 hours.

Serves 6

Low-fat Cassoulet

Olive oil spray

1 large eggplant, unpeeled, coarsely chopped

1 pound mushrooms, quartered

2 packages (10-oz. each) red pearl onions, peeled

4 carrots, chopped

1 large fennel bulb, trimmed and chopped

1 cup dry white wine

12 teaspoons assorted chopped fresh herbs such as thyme, rosemary, cilantro, basil—divided

7 large garlic cloves, minced

4 cups canned, seasoned crushed tomatoes with roasted garlic

2 cans (14^1/2-oz. each) low-salt chicken broth

1 cup lentils

1 pound low-fat smoked turkey sausage, coarsely chopped

2^1/2 cups fresh bread crumbs made from nonfat multi-grain bread (about 4 slices)

5 tablespoons fresh grated Parmesan cheese

Preheat oven to 350 degrees. Spray large heavy pot with olive oil spray. Heat over medium-high heat. Spray eggplant and mushrooms with olive oil spray and add to pot. Sauté until eggplant is tender and mushrooms are brown, about 15 minutes. Add onions, carrots, and fennel to pot. Sauté until carrots are almost tender, about 20 minutes. Add wine, 4 teaspoons herbs, and garlic. Simmer until wine is absorbed, about 4 minutes. Add tomatoes, broth, and lentils. Cover and simmer until lentils are just tender, about 20 minutes. Mix in sausage and 4 teaspoons herbs. Simmer until flavors blend but cassoulet is still juicy, about 4 minutes. Season with salt and pepper.

Mix bread crumbs, cheese, and remaining 4 teaspoons herbs in small bowl to blend. Transfer casserole to oven-safe dish. Top with bread crumb mixture and bake uncovered until filling bubbles and topping is crisp, about 30 minutes.   *Serves 6*

FLOUNDER WITH CITRUS SAUCE

2 oranges

4 fresh flounder fillets

2 teaspoons butter, melted

$^1/_4$ teaspoon paprika

Salt and pepper to taste

$^1/_2$ cup nonfat sour cream

2 tablespoons orange marmalade

$^1/_4$ teaspoon dried thyme

Peel oranges, remove pith, and slice into 8 slices. Set aside.

Place fish on greased rack of broiler pan. Combine butter, paprika, and salt and pepper to taste. Brush fish with butter mixture. Arrange orange slices around fish on broiler pan. Broil about 4 inches from heat for 4–6 minutes until fish flakes with a fork and orange slices are heated through. Remove from oven, cover with foil, and set aside.

Combine sour cream, marmalade, and thyme. Serve a dollop of mixture over each fish fillet.

Serves 4

COUSCOUS PILAF

$1^1/_2$ cups low-salt chicken broth

1 clove garlic, minced

1 cup couscous

$^1/_4$ cup currants

$^3/_4$ cup shredded spinach

$^1/_2$ cup shredded carrot

2 tablespoons finely chopped almonds

Combine chicken broth and garlic in large saucepan. Bring to boil. Stir in couscous and currants. Remove from heat. Cover and let stand 5 minutes. Fluff with fork. Stir in spinach, carrots, and almonds.   *Serves 4–6*

LENTIL AND ESCAROLE SOUP

1 tablespoon butter

$^1/_2$ onion, finely chopped

2 cloves garlic, finely chopped

1 carrot, coarsely chopped

$^3/_4$ cup lentils

1 bay leaf

3 whole canned tomatoes, drained, seeded, and coarsely chopped

1 teaspoon salt

$^1/_8$ teaspoon pepper

2 slices Italian bread, cut into cubes

1 teaspoon olive oil

$^1/_2$ head escarole, cut crosswise into 1-inch strips

Preheat oven to 425 degrees. Melt butter in large pot over medium heat. Add onion, garlic, and carrot and sauté until tender, about 5 minutes. Add lentils, bay leaf, tomatoes, salt, pepper, and 6 cups water. Bring to boil, reduce heat, and simmer until lentils are tender, about 40 minutes.

Place bread cubes on baking sheet and drizzle with olive oil. Toast in oven, turning occasionally, until golden brown, about 6 minutes.

Add escarole to soup and cook 5 more minutes. Serve topped with croutons.

Serves 4

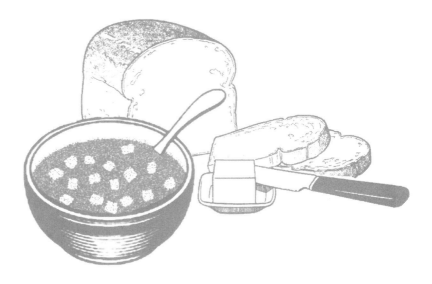

Bistro Garlic Chicken

1 bulb garlic (no, we don't mean clove, we mean bulb)

1 tablespoon olive oil

4 skinless, boneless chicken breast halves

$1/2$ teaspoon dried oregano

$1/2$ teaspoon dried thyme

$1/2$ teaspoon dried rosemary

$1/4$ teaspoon salt

$1/8$ teaspoon pepper

$1/4$ cup dry white wine

Preheat oven to 400 degrees. Separate cloves of garlic, discarding small papery cloves in center. Trim off stem end of each garlic clove, but do not peel.

Heat oil in large ovenproof skillet over medium-high heat until hot. Add garlic cloves and chicken. Cook 4 minutes or until chicken is lightly browned, turning chicken and stirring garlic cloves once. Sprinkle chicken with oregano, thyme, rosemary, salt, and pepper. Transfer skillet to oven. Bake, covered, for 12 to 15 minutes or until chicken is tender and no longer pink, and garlic is tender.

Transfer chicken to a serving platter, reserving juices in skillet. Keep warm. Transfer garlic cloves to small bowl. Set aside 1–2 minutes to cool slightly. Add wine to skillet. Squeeze softened garlic from skins into skillet. Discard skins. Bring to boil on range top. Reduce heat and boil gently, uncovered, until sauce thickens slightly, about 6 minutes, stirring frequently. Pour garlic sauce over chicken.

Serves 4

RYTA'S ABSOLUTELY GUILT-FREE TIRAMISÙ

$^1/_2$ cup sugar

1 cup nonfat Ricotta cheese

1 cup nonfat sour cream

2 tablespoons dark rum (or 1 teaspoon rum extract)

1 cup nonfat plain yogurt

1 teaspoon vanilla

1 package (8-oz.) light cream cheese (Neufchâtel)

$1^1/_4$ cups hot water

1 tablespoon plus 1 teaspoon instant espresso coffee

40 ladyfingers

$^1/_2$ teaspoon unsweetened cocoa

Process first seven ingredients in processor or blender. Combine hot water and espresso granules in small bowl. Split ladyfingers in half lengthwise. Quickly dip 20 ladyfinger halves cut side down in coffee. Place dipped side down into 13 x 9 x 2-inch baking dish. Dip 20 more; layer on top of first layer. Spread half of cheese mixture on top. Repeat procedure with ladyfinger halves, espresso, and cheese.

Randomly place toothpicks in Tiramisù to keep plastic wrap from sticking to cheese. Cover Tiramisù with plastic wrap. Chill 3–4 hours. Just before serving, sprinkle with cocoa.

Serves 20

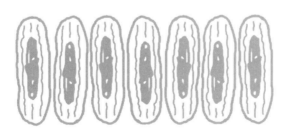

Light Crème Brûlée

2 eggs

2 egg whites

1/4 cup sugar

2 cups skim milk

1 teaspoon vanilla

1/8 teaspoon salt

2 tablespoons sugar

Preheat oven to 325 degrees. Combine eggs, egg whites, and 1/4 cup sugar in bowl. Beat with whisk until just combined. Add milk, vanilla, and salt. Mix well. Pour mixture into six 6-ounce custard cups. Place cups in large baking pan. Pour enough hot water into pan around cups to reach halfway up the sides of cups. Bake 40–50 minutes or until a knife inserted near center comes out clean. Remove custards from pan. Cool on wire rack. Cover and chill for at least 2 hours or overnight.

Remove custards from refrigerator. Let stand 20 minutes. Meanwhile, place 2 tablespoons sugar in small heavy skillet over medium-high heat until sugar begins to dissolve, shaking skillet occasionally. Do not stir. Once sugar starts to dissolve, reduce heat to low and cook about 5 minutes more or until all of sugar is melted and golden, stirring as needed with a wooden spoon. Quickly drizzle the caramelized sugar over custards. If sugar starts to harden in the skillet, return to heat, stirring until melted. Serve immediately. *Serves 6*

EASIEST AND MOST COMFORTING RICE PUDDING

Prepare **1 cup instant white rice** according to package directions. Prepare one **1-oz. package sugar-free, fat-free, instant vanilla pudding** according to package directions. When pudding is cool, add rice, and mix. Add **1/2 cup raisins**, if desired. Chill.

Good Girl Later ...

All right, writing a cookbook isn't the worst thing in the world. We could be doing crunches. The sun is shining in on our computer. We're each sitting next to our best friend. None of our combined six children has an ear infection. The health food store was well stocked with Evening Primrose Oil. And it's a pretty safe bet that neither of our husbands has planned a surprise romantic getaway at the Plaza for this weekend. Might as well write.

17 Mail-Nutrition
Food to Send to Summer Camp or College

Be creative—act, don't react.   —Dinkmeyer and McKay, RAISING A RESPONSIBLE CHILD

The instruction pamphlet from Camp Gotridayahaha commanded in large, italicized, bold print: *DO NOT EVER EVER SEND YOUR CAMPER FOOD OR WE WILL SEND YOUR CAMPER HOME SO YOU CAN TAKE CARE OF HIM/HER FOR EIGHT SCHOOL-LESS WEEKS! WE MEAN IT!*

During the seventeen-hour drive to the edge of the universe (where the camp was "conveniently located"), little Tasha perseverated: "Send me Hershey Bars send me pretzels send me ice cream send me salami send me Aunt Alice's meringues send me Hershey Bars."

Her mother, Moselle, rummaged through her purse for Advil, and kept her mind on her pending freedom. "Honey," cooed Moselle, "you know that parents are forbidden to send food to their children. It attracts vermin to the bunks, spoils in the mail, and melts in the July heat. Then you and your bunkmates will spend summer vacation throwing up. Is that what you want, sweetheart?"

"But Moooom! EEEEverybody gets care packages from home."

"I will send you packages, dear." Even though they were twelve hours into the trip, the Franklins were holding their tempers. Louis just kept his mind on negotiating the goat path the camp map called a road. After all, it wouldn't pay to arrive in Nameless Gorge, Nova Scotia with Tasha so agitated that she wouldn't get out of the car.

"Your 'permissible' packages are laaaaaaaaame. Last summer I used the crossword puzzle book under one leg of my cot to keep it from tilting. I gave that dumb stuffed crocodile to the nurse's baby. I threw away the stationery."

Moselle asked, "Are we there yet?"

WHAT TO SEND?

Camp and college care packages usually confine themselves to sweets. This mystifies us, for when kids are parent-free they are already creatively obtaining more sweets than they'd have at home. So, while we do include a neat bunch of mail-surviving dessert recipes, here is the hot tip of the century—a secret so well-kept that only the most grizzled of veteran camp parents are privy to it—send your child to camp with a can opener.

Yes! Care package non-sugar options are blown wide open. Canned vegetables, canned fruit, even canned soups and chilis … you'd be astonished at what kids will eat cold. (Most college dorms have microwave ovens available, though we have witnessed our own dorm resident forego them with straight-out-of-the-can machismo.)

And buy those sealed paper "cup of soup" cartons by the case. The only thing the camper needs for those is hot water. And those little over-priced individual pop-top tins of applesauce or fruit salad. The vistas are inebriating. So, while we're not ordinarily fans of processed foods, in Actual Real Life we figure a certain amount of it can't be any worse than a steady supply of UPS-ed sugar.

However, if you are concerned, all that canned produce, fruit, and chili have health-food store versions.

As for mailing sweets, there are four basic principles. Biscotti are less prone to breakage and crumbling than regular cookies: cookie bars keep their chocolate chips in better shape than regular cookies; frost nothing; and anything other than butter is a sturdier shortening. (The last two rules apply mainly to summer mailings, but it's always better to be safe than sorry.) And a suggestion: Send just enough for your camper, her bunkmates, and her counselors to demolish at one sitting; sweets attract bugs like the devil.

Pack in coffee cans with unsalted, dry (popped, but unbuttered) popcorn nestled between the baked goods. Then wrap the cans in bubble wrap, place in box surrounded by foam pellets or more popcorn, and send on to your joyously distant adolescent. Pay the impoverishing guaranteed two-day delivery rates. It's better than an entire bunk's parents accusing you of manslaughter.

DOUBLE CHERRY LINZER BARS

2 cups ground walnuts, divided

2 cups old-fashioned oatmeal, *uncooked*

1 cup flour

$^1/_4$ teaspoon salt

3 sticks ($1^1/_2$ cups) unsalted margarine, softened

$1^1/_2$ cups confectioners' sugar

2 eggs, lightly beaten

1 tablespoon vanilla

$1^1/_2$ cups cherry preserves or jam

$^3/_4$ cup dried cherries

1 heaping tablespoon grated orange zest

Preheat oven to 350 degrees. Lightly grease 13 x 9 x 2-inch pan. In mixing bowl, thoroughly combine $1^1/_2$ cups ground walnuts, oats, flour, and salt. Set aside.

Beat together margarine and confectioners' sugar until fluffy. Beat in eggs and vanilla. Stir in oat mixture. Take $1^1/_3$ cups of this oat-egg mixture and set aside.

Spread remaining oat-egg mixture in pan. Bake 15 minutes or until golden. Leaving oven on, cool pan 10 minutes on wire rack.

Meanwhile, combine preserves, cherries, and orange zest, and spread on crust. Stir remaining $^1/_2$ cup walnuts into reserved oat-egg mixture. Drop by spoonfuls evenly over jam. Bake 35 minutes or until golden. Cool thoroughly on rack. Cut into bars, wrap each bar in a square of waxed paper, and pack.

Makes 24 bars

BROWN SUGARS

1¹/₂ cups flour

¹/₂ cup light brown sugar, packed

1 tablespoon orange juice (or strong coffee if you have some left over)

¹/₄ teaspoon salt

1 stick unsalted margarine, chilled

Small bag (6-oz.) semisweet chocolate chips

2 eggs

1 cup dark brown sugar, packed

¹/₄ cup flour

¹/₄ teaspoon salt

¹/₂ teaspoon baking powder

1 teaspoon vanilla

1 cup chopped almonds, pecans, or nuts of your choice

Preheat oven to 375 degrees. Combine first four ingredients. Cut in margarine until mixture is crumbly. Press onto bottom of ungreased 9 x 13 x 2-inch pan. Bake 10 minutes. Remove from oven (leaving oven on), and sprinkle evenly with chocolate chips.

Using electric mixer, beat eggs until thick and increased in volume. Stir in the remaining ingredients. Spread this mixture gently over the chips. Bake an additional 20 minutes, or until golden. Cut into squares and pack.

Makes 24 bars

BROWNIE BISCOTTI

A bittersweet, dense treat. Moist and crisp simultaneously—where the American and Italian palates meet. If your children prefer, you may leave out the raisins or apricots, although they bring the recipe to the next level.

³/4 cup raisins *or* chopped dried apricots

³/4 cup warm water

3 eggs

1¹/4 cups sugar

4 tablespoons butter

10 ounces bittersweet or semisweet chocolate

6 tablespoons cocoa

2 teaspoons vanilla

3¹/2 cups flour, plus some extra for rolling

1 teaspoon baking powder

Preheat oven to 325 degrees, with rack in middle position. Line an oiled baking sheet with parchment paper. Plump apricots or raisins in warm water for 1 hour.

Beat eggs and sugar until fluffy. In small saucepan, melt butter, chocolate, and cocoa, then remove from heat and stir in vanilla. Cool a bit, then fold into egg-sugar mixture. Drain plumped fruit and stir in.

In separate bowl, combine flour and baking powder. Add to batter and beat until dough pulls away from sides of bowl. Flour your hands and work surface well, and roll dough into two 15-inch logs, each about 1¹/2 inches in diameter. Transfer logs to prepared sheet and bake about 30 minutes or very lightly browned and no longer soft. Cool until logs can be handled easily.

Using serrated knife, cut each log on the diagonal into ¹/2-inch wide slices. (Yes, traditional biscotti are sliced thinner, but this works better for care packages.) Return cookies to baking sheet cut side up, and bake an additional 10 minutes. *Makes about 2 dozen biscotti*

LEMON ALMOND BISCOTTI

If a cookie could ever be called refreshing, this might be it.

2 cups flour, plus some extra for rolling

1 teaspoon baking powder

$^1/_4$ teaspoon salt

3 tablespoons butter

1 cup sugar

2 eggs

$^1/_2$ teaspoon almond extract

2 tablespoons *fresh* lemon juice

4 teaspoons grated lemon zest

$^1/_2$ cup coarsely chopped almonds, lightly toasted

Preheat oven to 350 degrees, with rack in middle position. Line an oiled baking sheet with parchment paper. Put first three ingredients in small bowl and set aside. Beat butter and sugar until fluffy. Beat in eggs one at a time. Beat in almond extract, lemon juice, and zest. Stir in almonds. Transfer dry ingredients from small bowl to sifter or mesh sieve. Sift into the mixing bowl with egg mixture. Fold in dry ingredients until just combined.

With floured hands and work surface, divide dough in half, and roll into 2 logs about 2 inches thick and 1 foot long. Place on prepared sheet and flatten logs to a height of about $^3/_4$ inch. Bake 35 minutes. Cool 10 minutes.

Reduce oven temperature to 325 degrees. Using serrated knife, cut each log on the diagonal into $^1/_2$-inch slices. Return slices to baking sheet cut side up, and bake 6–8 minutes. Turn over cookies and bake a final 6–8 minutes, or until crisp and golden brown. Cool on wire rack.   *Makes about 3 dozen biscotti*

BOURBON HAZELNUT BROWNIES

While the previous treats are not by any means juvenile, here's one specifically for the faraway grown-ups on your list.

1¹/2 cups hazelnuts

¹/3 cup bourbon

4 squares unsweetened chocolate

1 stick butter *(We can't bear to make these with margarine. We delude ourselves into thinking booze preserves things.)*

3 eggs

1¹/4 cups sugar

1 cup flour

¹/2 teaspoon baking powder

¹/2 teaspoon salt

2 teaspoons vanilla

Soak hazelnuts in bourbon for 1 hour.

Preheat oven to 350 degrees. Grease and flour a 9 x 9-inch pan. Melt chocolate and butter; set aside. In mixing bowl, beat eggs until slightly thickened. Add sugar gradually, beating well between additions. Beat in chocolate-butter mixture.

In separate bowl, stir together flour, baking powder, and salt. Add to mixing bowl and beat to combine. Stir in vanilla, soaked nuts, and any unabsorbed bourbon. Pour batter into prepared pan. Bake 20 minutes.

Cool, slice, and wrap each square in delicately-shaded tissue paper, unless you are sending to a male in the military, in which case waxed paper will be safer. To keep moist, poke a few tiny holes in a small plastic bag. Place a half of an apple inside and tie securely. Put this bag in the container with your brownies.

Makes one dozen

LATER ...

On visiting day, not only Tasha, but thirty-two grateful children ran down the hill to the mud parking lot to greet Louis and Moselle. The camp director neither scolded nor criticized Moselle for her "illegal" packages. He simply handed her an application for next summer and kept his mind on her deposit.

18 Sauté Over Medium Fame
Meals That Will Make You Feel Like You're at the Oscars

As the result of the poverty of modern life, we are confronted with the circumstance that art is more interesting than life. —Robert Motherwell

"Life is good. I am good. Good is good. Life is good. I am good. Good is good." Craig was not Gregory Peck, and he couldn't get over it. But now, after fifty years of wanting to be larger than life, Craig (himself a psychologist), with the help of two therapists and a tsunami of self-help books, was finally learning that life is precious even when the paparazzi leave you alone. Lying on his natural fiber meditation mat with all his muscles in a state of complete relaxation (which took three years of intense labor to accomplish), he chanted his mantra.

In years past, Craig spent the weeks preceding Oscar night engaged in Lucy Riccardo-inspired schemes to finagle a ticket to the festivities. One year he secured a custodial position at Price-Waterhouse, certain he could search the jacket pockets of the officials who tally the votes, and "find a stray ticket." Four months in prison did nothing to dissuade him from trying again. Last year he discovered that his high school drama teacher's butcher butterflied the lamb for Kevin Costner's manicurist's birthday bash. No luck.

But this year Craig was mentally healthy. He and Betsy, with a flourish of ceremony, withdrew the equivalent of his annual Screen Actors Guild dues, and went directly to Circuit City where they purchased a television the size of Kevin Costner's manicurist's house. This year he was going to the Oscars! And all his friends would be with him.

What to serve?

Sushi Hors d'Oeuvres

Sushi is *de rigueur* in all the "hip" places right now, particularly among those wanting to look as though their size-four gowns were melted onto them. We recommend ordering a platter of **cucumber rolls** and **California rolls** from your local Japanese restaurant. They are easily popped into the mouth and neither contains the raw fish that may repel some of your guests.

Wild and Brown Rice Pancakes with Sour Cream and Caviar

Following the instructions on the box of **wild and brown rice**, make the amount of rice appropriate to your guest count. When rice has cooled, add **1 beaten egg** for every 6 servings of rice and mix well. Pour **olive oil** into large skillet to about $1/4$ inch deep. Drop tablespoon-size portions of the rice mixture into the oil and press with the back of the spoon to form thin pancakes. Fry until golden and pancakes don't fall apart, turning over once. Drain pancakes on paper towels. Serve with a dollop of **sour cream** and a spoonful of **caviar** on each pancake.

OVEN-DRIED TOMATOES AND GOAT CHEESE CROSTINI

These tomatoes are better than diamonds. Don't even think about substituting the store-bought sun-dried ones for these tomatoes. Once you taste ours you will understand why there is no turning back.

Preheat oven to 200 degrees. Wash and thoroughly dry as many **ripe plum tomatoes** as you can stand washing and drying in one day. Cut them in half lengthwise and place them cut side up on cookie sheets. Sprinkle with **salt and pepper**. Mince 6 cloves of **garlic** per 20 tomatoes and sprinkle liberally. Place a **fresh basil leaf** on each tomato. Lightly drizzle **olive oil** over tomatoes. Bake for 10–12 hours until tomatoes are dry but not totally lifeless and shriveled. We let the tomatoes cook while we sleep. In the morning the kitchen smells like our fantasy farmhouse in Tuscany.

By themselves the tomatoes will last in a covered jar in the refrigerator for a few days. If you immerse them in **olive oil**, cover the jar and refrigerate, they will last for 2 weeks. (Include those blackened basil leaves, if you wish.)

CROSTINI: Thinly slice a **baguette**. Brush each slice with **olive oil** and rub with **garlic**. Toast. Spread **goat cheese** which has been brought to room temperature over each toasted slice. Top with **dried tomatoes**.

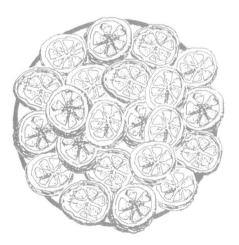

OVEN-ROASTED SALMON WITH CITRUS SAUCE

SAUCE:

3/4 cup fresh orange juice

1/2 cup balsamic vinegar

2 anchovy fillets, finely minced

2 tablespoons thinly sliced scallions

2 teaspoons each minced fresh basil and parsley

2 tablespoons minced orange zest

1/8 teaspoon salt

Freshly ground black pepper

SALMON:

2 tablespoons olive oil

Four 6-ounce salmon fillets

Salt

Freshly ground black pepper

Preheat oven to 450 degrees. Combine all sauce ingredients in a glass jar. Cover tightly and shake. Set aside.

Heat olive oil in large skillet over high heat. Season fish with salt and pepper. Place fillets in skillet skin side down, and transfer skillet to the oven. Roast 8–10 minutes until medium rare or longer, if desired.

Heat sauce in small saucepan. Spoon sauce over salmon and serve. *Serves 4*

PAN ROASTED BABY RED POTATOES

15 baby red potatoes

3 tablespoons olive oil

1 garlic clove, peeled and crushed

1 teaspoon kosher salt

I tablespoon fresh chopped rosemary

1 tablespoon fresh chopped thyme

Wash but do not peel potatoes. Place them in heavy large skillet in which you have heated olive oil. Cook 25 minutes on low heat, occasionally rolling pan to evenly brown potatoes. Add garlic, salt, rosemary, and thyme. Cover and cook until done, about 10 more minutes. *Serves 4–5*

PISTACHIO-CRUSTED CHICKEN BREASTS WITH HERBED CHEESE FILLING

This chicken can be made a day in advance and reheated, leaving you free to sit in front of the television if you wish to serve during, instead of before, the show.

HERBED GARLIC CHEESE FILLING:

8 ounces softened cream cheese *(The fat-free variety tastes fine in this dish.)*

1 teaspoon minced garlic

1 tablespoon chopped parsley

1–2 tablespoons minced fresh basil

1/4 teaspoon salt

Pepper to taste

CHICKEN:

8 boneless, skinless chicken breast halves

1/2 cup flour mixed with 1 teaspoon each salt and pepper

2 eggs, beaten

1 1/2 cups finely ground pistachio nuts (about 7 ounces shelled)

1/4 cup olive oil

Combine all Filling ingredients. Chill until firm and form into eight 2-inch long cylinders. Refrigerate until ready to use.

Preheat oven to 350 degrees. Pound chicken breasts between two pieces of waxed paper until each is 1/4-inch thick. Place 1 cheese cylinder along the edge of each breast and roll and fold until the cheese is completely encased in the chicken breast.

Roll each piece first in flour, then in beaten eggs, and finally in ground pistachios. Sauté in olive oil over medium heat for 1–2 minutes on each side until lightly browned. Transfer chicken to baking pan and bake for an additional 20 minutes. Serve hot. *Serves 8*

POTATO AND LEEK PURÉE

This recipe can be made a day in advance.

6 large leeks

2 pounds Yukon Gold potatoes

1 stick butter (Hey, it's the Oscars!)

2 garlic cloves, minced

$1/2$ cup milk (skim works, but whole or 2 percent is better), heated

Salt and pepper to taste

Trim roots and most of green leaves from leeks. Split down to the base but do not cut through. Rinse thoroughly. Bring 3 quarts salted water to a boil. Add leeks and cook until tender, about 15 minutes. Drain and chop.

While leeks are boiling, peel potatoes. Cover them with cold water in a separate pot. Add salt and bring to a boil. Reduce heat and cook until potatoes are very tender, 20–40 minutes depending on their size. Drain and reserve.

Melt 3 tablespoons butter in a skillet. Add garlic and cook over low heat until lightly colored, about 10 minutes. Add leeks and another 3 tablespoons butter and sauté for 10 more minutes. Transfer leeks and garlic to food processor and purée until smooth. Mash potatoes *by hand* adding heated milk as needed. Stir in leek purée and remaining 2 tablespoons butter, melted. Season with salt and pepper.

Serves 6

Sautéed Broccoli Rabe with Garlic

**2 pounds broccoli rabe washed, largest
   stems discarded**

3 tablespoons olive oil

2 teaspoons finely minced garlic

$1/3$ teaspoon dried red pepper flakes

$1/2$ teaspoon salt

Freshly ground black pepper

$3/4$ cup water

4 lemon wedges

Olive oil

Chop broccoli rabe into 2- to 3-inch pieces. In skillet large enough to hold all of the broccoli rabe, combine olive oil, garlic, and red pepper flakes. Cook over moderate heat until oil is flavored but garlic is not browned. Add broccoli rabe. Toss continuously 1–2 minutes until wilted. Add salt and pepper, toss, and cook 1 minute longer. Add water and cook until tender 3–5 minutes. Serve on warm platter with lemon wedges and drizzle olive oil over top.

Serves 6–8

Asparagus Vinaigrette

VINAIGRETTE:

1 tablespoon Dijon mustard

4 tablespoons balsamic vinegar

1 teaspoon granulated sugar

$1/2$ teaspoon salt

$1/4$ teaspoon pepper

Snipped fresh chives

$1/3$ cup olive oil

ASPARAGUS:

$1 1/2$ pounds asparagus

Mix all Vinaigrette ingredients together except olive oil. Slowly pour olive oil into mix while whisking constantly.

Cut $1/2$ inch off bottom of each asparagus stalk. Steam or microwave as desired.

Pour Vinaigrette over cooked asparagus.

Serves 6

Extreme Lemon Tart with Berry Sauce

Yes, this recipe is very fattening, but it's too late to look like Julia Roberts now anyway, so get festive, enjoy, and fast tomorrow. The calories in this tart are worth it!

SHELL:

$1^3/4$ cups flour

$1/3$ cup sugar

9 tablespoons cold butter

1 egg

FILLING:

$1^2/3$ cups lemon juice (9 lemons)

$1/4$ cup plus 3 tablespoons fresh lemon zest (peeled off the 9 lemons)

7 large eggs

1 cup heavy cream

$1^3/4$ cups sugar

SAUCE:

$2^1/2$ cups fresh raspberries

2 cups fresh strawberries

$1/2$ cup sugar

$2/3$ cup water

Optional: **sweetened whipped cream**

*When using dried beans as weights, do not discard; they may be used multiple times. But do make sure to label their container— they are no longer fit for eating.

Preheat oven to 400 degrees. Put flour and sugar into food processor and pulse until mixed. Add butter and pulse until coarse meal is formed. Add egg and pulse until a ball of dough is formed. If the dough doesn't form a ball, add a little cold water. Remove dough from processor, wrap in plastic wrap, and chill 1 hour.

Roll out dough and place in 8-inch tart pan that is at least 3 inches deep. Line shell with foil and pour dried beans or rice on top of foil to keep dough from rising or bubbling. Place pan in oven and bake 10 minutes. Remove foil with the beans or rice, and discard.* Bake crust for 8–9 more minutes. Cool on rack.

Whisk all Filling ingredients together and cook in saucepan over medium heat until thickened. Pour into tart shell. Return to middle rack of oven for 30 minutes. Transfer tart pan to rack to cool. Chill tart in refrigerator until ready to serve.

Mix all Sauce ingredients together in heavy saucepan and cook over high heat until boiling. Remove from heat and let stand 10 minutes. Strain liquid from berries. Boil liquid until syrup is reduced to $3/4$ cup. Add berries and cool completely.

Serve tart with Berry Sauce and a dollop of whipped cream, if desired.   *Serves 8–10*

ELEGANT AND EASY BAKED APPLES

These are just as gorgeous when made a day ahead and reheated in the oven—not the microwave!

1 Granny Smith or Winesap apple per guest

Butter

Sugar and cinnamon mixed

Raisins

Store-bought ready-to-bake pie crusts (Use $^3/_4$ of a crust per apple, plus extra for top)

Beaten eggs

Crushed almonds

Vanilla ice cream

Preheat oven to 425 degrees. Core but do not peel apples. Peel a $^1/_2$-inch rim around top of each apple. Insert one small pat butter into opening. Add 1 teaspoon sugar and cinnamon mixture and a few raisins. Wrap $^3/_4$ of a whole pie crust around each apple encasing it completely. After 3 apples, you will have enough crust to roll together for a 4th apple.

Roll out one additional pie crust with a rolling pin. Using a scalloped pastry cutter, cut $^1/_4$-inch-wide strips of dough. Crisscross two strips on top of each apple. Brush each apple with beaten egg. Sprinkle some crushed almonds which have been added to the remaining sugar and cinnamon mixture, over each apple. Bake at 425 for 10 minutes. Reduce heat to 350 and bake for an additional 45 minutes. The apples should be nicely browned. If they begin to burn, cover loosely with foil while continuing to bake. Serve warm with vanilla ice cream.

LATER ...

No one heard the acceptance speech for Best Sound Editing because the guests were applauding the Oven-Dried Tomato and Goat Cheese Crostini. Best Screenplay was overshadowed by moans of ecstasy over the Extreme Lemon Tart. And Craig silently awarded himself the Oscar for Best Actor ... for so ably impersonating a psychologically sound guy who didn't care that he wasn't a Player at the real Oscar ceremonies.

But Craig is a true endeavorer on the path to self- and reality-acceptance. As soon as he and Betsy dried the crystal, he boarded his natural fiber mat and intoned, "The hors d'oeuvres were good. The salmon was good. The dessert was good. Life is good."

19 Renovation Starvation
Cooking Without a Kitchen

A bowl and a knife, a bowl and a knife. All one needs to create a banquet for Mandarins is a bowl and a knife. — SHARON SIMPLIFIES

The realtor didn't even want to show them the house. "It's a dump. Too old. You have four teenagers and there's only one bathroom. And the kitchen! The kitchen was hit by lightening in 1928, and hasn't been touched since."

Sight unseen, Mariko and Dan Tsui knew it would be perfect. Dan could now justify buying macho tools and drawing blueprints when he wasn't selling Saturns. With some patience, Mariko would have the custom kitchen and house of her dreams.

Joy, Leigh, Howard, and Dan Jr. had always tolerated the idiotic fantasies of their parents. But tolerance does not fill the hollow legs of four behemoths.

Before the family even unpacked, they set up a "kitchen." The 1948 Frigidaire was still operational, until they moved it into the living room—where it became sculpture. So they purchased a mini-fridge to hold the ice cubes and milk during the renovation, and which could later travel to college with Leigh. They plugged in their microwave and toaster oven, borrowed a two-burner electric hot plate, and set up their other bare necessity, the imported Fraushtupt Automatic Bean-Grinding Milk-Steaming Self-Timing Combination Latté Espresso Cappuccino Maker. After placing dishwashing liquid and dishtowels by the bathtub, they were ready to cook.

What to serve?

Tips for Shopping and Coping

1. No matter the size of your family, this is one time you should not shop in bulk. With limited refrigerator space, you are going to find yourself shopping daily. There is no way to get around it: Feel European.

2. Even if it's been your turn for the last six months to entertain your friends or family, presume just a bit longer. Conversely, call in all your chits—beg for dinner invitations, and offer to contribute in the ways you can, despite renovation. Menu-plan, shop, help cook in your friend's kitchen, and of course help with clean-up.

3. There are certain foods that are technically items which need refrigeration, but which actually can be bought the day they will be eaten, and left on a shelf for several hours:

   Individual yogurts

   Fruits and vegetables (especially those veggies which will be cooked)

   Processed lunch meats (if the weather is not sweltering)

   Cheeses (which actually should be served at room temperature)

   Remember: Except for the fruit, if you've deprived these items of refrigeration, either eat them within 18 hours or ditch them.

4. Although you may be philosophically opposed to BurgerMaven, knuckle under once a week. Gain a new-found respect for your local pizzeria. Traditional "take-out" establishments are your handiest option, and some are currently providing tables. Check out your nearest bagel shop. And throw in a few real restaurants if your budget permits. But since this is a cookbook, here is our *modus operandus* for renovation cuisine: Keep it simple, sweetie. One pot or skillet on your hot-plate. Disposable everything. Salads. Few ingredients. AND EASY CLEAN-UP.

5. You'll notice a curious omission of appetizer, soup, and dessert recipes in this chapter. We believe people who concoct full course dinners *sans* kitchen are masochistic. They are not looking for practical advice about Actual Real Life and therefore are probably not reading this book. For normal people we have included simple recipes for salads and entrées. For Pete's sake and your own, buy Twinkies if you can't live without dessert.

SALADE NIÇOISE

2 large baking potatoes (about
  1¹/4 pounds)

Salted water

³/4 pound frozen French-cut green beans
  (*We only suggest using frozen when
  simplicity is paramount.*)

1 head Boston or romaine lettuce

2 cans (9¹/4-oz. each) water-packed
  tuna, well-drained

Salt and pepper to taste

1 cucumber, thinly sliced

1 can (2-oz.) flat anchovy fillets

¹/2 cup pitted ripe olives, halved

3 hard-cooked eggs, cut in wedges

2 tomatoes, cut in wedges

VINAIGRETTE:

¹/4 cup chopped parsley

1 garlic clove, crushed

¹/4 cup chopped onion

¹/4 cup red wine vinegar

2 tablespoons lemon juice

1 teaspoon Dijon mustard

¹/8 teaspoon sugar

¹/2 teaspoon dried basil

¹/2 cup olive oil

¹/2 cup vegetable oil

Salt and pepper to taste

Place unpeeled potatoes in medium saucepan. Cover with salted water. Cook uncovered until barely tender when pierced with a fork. Rinse under cold water to stop cooking. Let cool. Slice.

Defrost beans. Blanch in boiling water for 1 minute. Arrange lettuce on large platter. Arrange potato slices in single layer over lettuce. Decorate platter with remaining ingredients in whatever pattern you like. Or keep it simple and layer everything. Dress with Vinaigrette and serve with French bread.

VINAIGRETTE: Mix all ingredients in blender and whisk well. May be refrigerated for up to two weeks. Or buy pre-made dressing.

Serves 8, or 6 if two people are teenagers

Low Effort Chicken Quesadillas

2 pounds boneless, skinless, thin-sliced chicken breasts

Cajun seasoning to taste

3 tablespoons olive oil

Olive oil cooking spray

8 soft flour tortillas

1 cup shredded Cheddar cheese

Cut chicken breasts into bite-sized pieces. Sprinkle chicken liberally with Cajun seasoning. Sauté in olive oil until cooked through. Wipe out sauté pan. Coat clean pan with olive oil cooking spray.

Place one tortilla in pan. Place a generous portion of chicken on the tortilla. Sprinkle liberally with cheese and cover with a second tortilla. Spray the top of second tortilla with cooking spray. Flip quesadilla over after 2 minutes and cook for 1 minute more or until cheese is melted and tortilla is crisp. Slice as you would a pizza. Serve with salsa, sour cream, or guacamole, if desired.   *Serves 4*

No Effort Bean and Feta Quesadillas

1 can (16-oz.) refried beans

4 tablespoons chopped green onions

1 can (4-oz.) diced green chiles

8 soft flour tortillas

1$^{1}/_{2}$ cups crumbled Feta cheese

Olive oil cooking spray

In medium sized bowl mix together refried beans, green onions, and chiles. Spread $^{1}/_{2}$ of mixture on each of 4 tortillas. Sprinkle $^{1}/_{4}$ of Feta cheese over each and top with another tortilla. Coat large pan with cooking spray. Add the quesadilla. Cook 2 minutes, spray the top tortilla with cooking oil spray and flip it over. Cook for an additional 2 minutes or until cheese melts and tortillas are crisp. Follow same procedure for remaining 3 quesadillas. Slice as you would pizzas.   *Serves 4*

Black Bean, Red Pepper, and Corn Salad

1 can (16-oz.) black beans

1 can (11-oz.) corn niblets

4 tablespoons chopped green onions

1 red pepper, chopped

2 tablespoons olive oil

$^1/_3$ cup balsamic vinegar

Optional: **$^1/_2$ tablespoon chopped cilantro**

Combine all ingredients and serve. *Serves 8*

Spinach Salad with Mango and Jicama

DRESSING:

4 tablespoons orange juice

2 teaspoons white wine vinegar

$^1/_2$ teaspoon Dijon mustard

1 teaspoon chopped, fresh basil

Salt and pepper to taste

SALAD:

2 ripe mangoes, peeled and sliced

8 cups cut fresh spinach leaves

$^1/_2$ pound peeled, diced jicama

Whisk together all Dressing ingredients in small bowl. Set aside.

Toss the salad with the dressing. *Serves 8*

BROCCOLI WITH HONEY MUSTARD SAUCE

1 pound broccoli florets

1 tablespoon honey

1 tablespoon Dijon mustard

1 teaspoon lemon juice

4 tablespoons water

Salt and pepper to taste

Boil broccoli in salted water until tender about 2 minutes. Drain. Shock by dropping the broccoli into ice water. Drain well. Combine remaining ingredients in a small bowl and whisk together. Toss broccoli with this dressing.

Serves 4

ONE-PAN SHRIMP WITH TOMATOES, VERMOUTH, AND FETA

2 pounds large, peeled shrimp

3 tablespoons olive oil

1 cup vermouth

4 large, ripe, tomatoes, diced

1 cup crumbled Feta cheese

Sauté shrimp in olive oil until pink and almost cooked through. Add vermouth. Simmer for 2 minutes. Add tomatoes and simmer 1 more minute. Add Feta cheese and heat until warm. Serve alone or over rice or pasta.   *Serves 4*

POACHING FISH

When ovenless, don't forget about poaching. Fish poached in the microwave in water with lemon, or in white wine, is flaky and delicious. Poach salmon, trout, sea bass, or striped bass in a microwave-safe baking dish. Salt and pepper to taste or add your favorite fresh herbs. Serve with microwaved veggies and rice.

LATER ...

The Tsuis received the bill for the commercial refrigerator while spreading a perfect room temperature Gruyère on their bakery's lovely tomato-pignoli baguettes. After consuming the ethereal One-Pan Shrimp with Tomatoes, Vermouth, and Feta cooked on their camping hot-plate, they measured their wall space, and found they could not accommodate the mandatory vent for their restaurant range—without sacrificing the only functioning bathroom on the first floor. While Mariko munched on her healthy veggie boboli made in the toaster oven, she contemplated how truly fine her family had eaten during this time of "primitive" conditions. She briefly considered a more modest renovation. Very briefly.

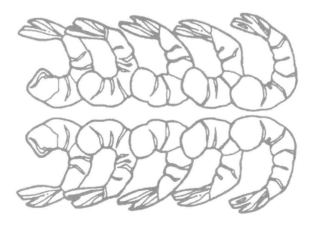

20 Now That You Flounder, Never Let Her Go
Food as Bait

Love is an ideal woven on the loom of the real. — George Bernard Shaw

In the new millennium we should be beyond tacky seduction tactics, but the most we've managed to accomplish is to give men equal opportunity for exhausting themselves, chapping their hands, and palpitating with fear of rejection of both one's purest self and one's puffiest soufflé. Male or female, the neophyte cook's first attempt at a pull-out-all-the-stops meal is fraught with earnestness complicated by ignorance and inexperience.

Publications not having caught up with society, John couldn't find an article in GQ entitled, "How To Lure Her Into Permanent Commitment With This Romantic and Irresistible Valentine's Supper-By-Candlelight." He had to resort to *Cosmopolitan*.

John, leafing through *Cosmo*, thinking: A big, juicy T-bone. That's always special. Oh damn, she'll think that's guy food. I've got to come off sensitive ... New Age ... an enlightened, health-conscious wuss kind of guy. Vegetarian: No slaughtering Bambi! Naaah, if I lead her to believe that green things are acceptable as main dishes, she may expect me to do something really outrageous ... like going for a walk. That leaves chicken or fish. Crap. Ma used to slide her entire arm up the butt and pull out the most sick looking shit. I cannot finger chicken guts.

So it looks like fish. The most politically correct breathing thing. It's not cute so you don't care about killing it. It doesn't have calories or fat. The guy behind the counter knifes out all the ugly stuff. It cooks fast leaving me time to impress Angela with my wit and unique perspective on ... everything.

What to serve?

Easy Hot Crab Dip

1 package (8-oz.) cream cheese

1 tablespoon mayonnaise (may be low-fat or fat-free)

2 tablespoons white wine

1 teaspoon Dijon mustard

^{1}/2 teaspoon sugar

^{1}/4 teaspoon salt

1 can (7 ^{1}/2-oz.) crabmeat

^{1}/2 cup slivered almonds

Preheat oven to 350 degrees. In large bowl combine all ingredients, except almonds. Transfer to soufflé dish and bake until warm. Toast almonds in toaster-oven and sprinkle on top of warm dip. Serve with crackers or a sliced baguette.   *Serves many*

Five Additional Ideas for Easy Hors d'Oeuvres

1. Wrap **cubes of melon** in strips of **thinly sliced prosciutto** and skewer with toothpicks.

2. Spread a thin layer of **olive oil** and purchased **pesto** on slices of **French baguette**. Top with **sun-dried tomatoes** and **fresh Mozzarella**. Broil until cheese melts.

3. Brush **large mushroom caps** with **olive oil**, fill with pieces of **Brie cheese**, top with a **basil leaf** and bake for 10 minutes at 350 degrees.

4. Thinly slice **black bread**. Spread slices with **Boursin cheese**. Top with **thin slices of rare roast beef**.

5. Blanch **asparagus spears** in boiling water for 1 minute. Cool and wrap each spear in a **slice of pancetta**. Serve with your favorite **vinaigrette**.

EASY BAKED FLOUNDER IN MASHED POTATO CRUST

1 lemon

1 cup frozen mashed potatoes, thawed

2 large scallions, chopped

1 teaspoon dried thyme

Two 5–6 ounce flounder fillets (other white fish such as orange roughy may be substituted)

2 teaspoons butter

¹/₂ cup fresh bread crumbs

Salt and pepper to taste

Preheat oven to 450 degrees. Line a baking sheet with foil and grease the foil. Grate enough peel from the lemon to measure 1 teaspoon. Mix mashed potatoes, scallions, thyme, and lemon peel in medium bowl until well blended. Season with salt and pepper. Arrange fish on prepared sheet. Season fish with salt and pepper and squeeze some lemon juice over fillets. Spread half of potato mixture over each fish fillet, covering completely.

Melt butter in heavy skillet over medium heat. Add bread crumbs and toss until evenly coated. Spoon crumbs over potato crusts, dividing equally and pressing to adhere. Bake fish until just cooked through and potato crusts and crumbs are beginning to brown, about 20 minutes. *Serves 2*

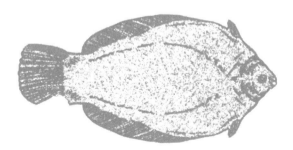

VERY EASY FILLET OF FLOUNDER (OR SOLE) IN PIQUANT TOMATO SAUCE

²/3 cup thinly sliced yellow onion

4 tablespoons olive oil

2 teaspoons finely chopped garlic

1¹/2 teaspoons dried oregano

3 tablespoons capers

1 cup canned Italian tomatoes, cut up, with their juice

Salt and pepper to taste

2 pounds fresh fillet of flounder or sole

Preheat oven to 450 degrees. Sauté onion with olive oil in medium skillet over medium heat until soft and light brown. Add garlic, and when it begins to brown, add oregano and capers, stirring once or twice. Add tomatoes and their juice, salt, and pepper. Stir well and simmer 15 to 20 minutes or until tomatoes and oil separate.

Rinse fish fillets in cold water and blot dry. Spray large baking dish with cooking oil spray. Smear bottom with about 1 tablespoon of tomato mixture. Dip each fillet into sauce so both sides of fish have been coated, then arrange fillets in a single layer in the baking dish. Pour remaining sauce over fillets and place dish on highest oven rack. Cook for no more than 5 to 8 minutes or fillets will become dry. If sauce has thinned, remove baking dish from oven, transfer fish to serving dish, pour sauce into a saucepan and heat until sauce thickens.   *Serves 4*

Super-Easy-Lip-Smacking Honey-Lemon Chicken

This recipe serves four, but freezes well. You'll want the leftovers for lunch.

4 each, chicken thighs and drumsticks or equivalent in pieces you prefer

2 tablespoons butter or margarine, melted

^{1}/3 cup flour

1 teaspoon salt

^{1}/4 teaspoon pepper

^{1}/3 cup honey

^{1}/4 cup lemon juice

1 tablespoon soy sauce

Preheat oven to 400 degrees. Brush chicken with butter, then dredge with flour which has been seasoned with salt and pepper. Place skin side down on lightly oiled, foil-lined pan or easy-to-clean baking dish. (This chicken can get sticky. It is the only recipe which we suggest cooking in a disposable foil pan.) Bake 30 minutes. Remove from oven and turn over chicken.

Mix remaining ingredients and pour ^{1}/2 of mixture over chicken parts. Bake 20 minutes, then baste again with more sauce and bake for another 10 minutes. Baste one more time and cook 10 more minutes. Chicken should be nicely browned and coated. *Serves 4*

You Won't Believe How Easy Hearts of Palm Salad with Tomato and Onion

^{1}/4 cup olive oil

3 tablespoons chopped fresh basil or 2 teaspoon dried basil

2 tablespoons white wine vinegar

1 pound plum tomatoes, cut into wedges

1 can (14 oz.) hearts of palm, drained, cut crosswise into 1-inch pieces

1 medium onion, thinly sliced

Whisk oil, basil, and vinegar in medium bowl to blend. Add remaining ingredients and toss to blend. Season to taste with salt and pepper. Let salad stand at room temperature at least 30 minutes or up to 2 hours. *Serves 4*

STILL EASY BUT RUNNING OUT OF TITLES ARUGULA AND RED PEPPER SALAD

**1 head of leafy green lettuce such as
   romaine or Boston**

1 bunch of arugula

$1/2$ pound shiitake mushrooms

1 large red bell pepper

$1/2$ of 14-oz. can artichoke hearts

Wash all lettuce and remove stems from
arugula. Remove stems from mushrooms and
wash. Toss all ingredients together and drizzle
with Balsamic Vinaigrette (below).   *Serves 6*

BALSAMIC VINAIGRETTE

1 tablespoon Dijon mustard

3 tablespoons balsamic vinegar

Salt and freshly ground pepper to taste

1 cup extra virgin olive oil

1 garlic clove, peeled and chopped

Whisk mustard and vinegar together in small
bowl. Season with salt and pepper. Dribble oil
into bowl in a slow steady stream while whisking constantly until dressing is creamy and all
oil has been used. Add garlic and stir.

Makes $1^1/2$ cups

EASIEST LIME PIE EVER

3 eggs, separated

$1/3$ to $1/2$ cup fresh lime juice

1 can (14-oz.) sweetened condensed milk

**One 9-inch purchased graham cracker
   pie crust**

Preheat oven to 250 degrees. In large bowl, beat
egg whites until stiff. In separate bowl, combine
the 3 yolks, lime juice, and condensed milk. Fold
into the egg whites until thoroughly combined.
Pour mixture into pie crust and bake for
10 minutes.   *Serves 8*

Marilyn's World's Easiest Chocolate Cake That's Not a Mix

1 cup sugar

1 stick margarine

4 eggs

1 teaspoon vanilla

1 can Hershey's or other chocolate syrup

1 cup flour

1 teaspoon baking powder

Confectioners' sugar

Preheat oven to 325 degrees. Cream sugar and margarine. Add eggs and vanilla. Stir in chocolate. Add flour and baking powder. Pour batter into a greased tube pan. Batter will be very thin. Bake 50 minutes. Remove sides of pan immediately. Cool completely. Gently slide knife between cake and pan bottom, loosening cake completely. Hold upside down and slide cake from pan. Transfer cake to plate and sprinkle with confectioners' sugar.   *Serves 10*

Later ...

Angela, thirty years later, thinking: Three hundred sixty-five multiplied by thirty—I've cooked enough meat and potato dinners to feed two generations of NFL teams. What a sucker I was. But that Fillet of Flounder was so divine and John was so sincere about not killing Bambi, how could I have said anything but yes to his proposal? Plus, there was my two-carat Van Cleef and Arpel marquis-cut floating in my Moet and Chandon. So what if he never set foot in the kitchen again except to get a glass of water for a Tylenol? He vacuums like a Midwestern tornado. He does all the grocery shopping: He's so valiant, hauling in those weighty bags of standing rib roasts.

Besides, between the Wamsuttas he's a man that even the *Cosmo* Girl couldn't imagine. How could I begrudge my Johnny his iron?

21 Leaven-Worth
Accommodating a Multitude of Health Restrictions on Passover

The best form of prayer is work. —Israel Zangwill

Don't let the title fool you into thinking we have any reserves of humor for this chapter. A normal Passover is labor enough. Any Jewish, and many regular cookbooks, will give you regulations, ideas, and recipes for wheatless, flourless, yeastless, riceless, pastaless, and legumeless cuisine. What they rarely provide are recipes free of all-of-the-above for (soy-less!) vegetarian meals, for low-fat meals during a time of above-normal flesh consumption, and for diabetic-fit sugarless cooking during this festive eight days.

We assume our readers are people who buy cookbooks and therefore already own resources for preparing traditional holiday meals, including Passover. But this particular holiday predicament, although unfortunately common and becoming more so as our population ages and ails, is almost never addressed: How to cook with strict religious circumscriptions complicated by equally strict health circumscriptions?

The question now having been posed, here is our humorless, unimaginative, really brief story set-up:

Passover was coming; Dina Katz wondered if it would truly hurt to shoot herself in the head.

What to serve?

Suggestions for a Nutritionally Demanding Passover

1. Roast a turkey or turkey breast. You know how; just remember not to salt it, oil it, or baste it with drippings. Simply season with herbs. With skin removed *after cooking,* this is a fine main dish for all except the vegetarians.

2. So that vegetarians can enjoy the stuffing, keep it separate from the poultry. (Unless you are making two—and if you are, we've included a recipe for those allergic to wheat, that does go inside the turkey.)

3. Prepare mashed potatoes with Mother's Margarine which is kosher for Passover. Instead of combining with pounds of sautéed onions (a traditional dish at our more indulgent seders), mash with roasted garlic which uses little or no oil.

4. Do not cook anything with salt. Bring salt to the table for those rare individuals who have the incredible good fortune to be allowed food that tastes like anything. The one exception to this rule is the soup. Chicken or vegetarian broths are disgusting without salt. Torture only those who demand it: Separate salted and unsalted batches.

5. Matzoh balls made with egg beaters turn out fine, as does Matzoh Brie (egg-fried Matzoh).

6. Serve an overflowing mixed green salad which everyone may eat. Even though there are Passover-fit bottled dressings, skip the chemicals. Make a homemade dressing using lemon juice and herbs, and go light on the oil. Ta da! Balsamic vinegar now comes kosher for Passover. A big fruit salad is also welcome by all except the diabetics, who will be enjoying the aforementioned green salad.

7. Other recipes from this book which may prove useful are Elegant Sweet Potatoes with Cointreau and Cherries (page 25), Med-Med Soup (page 132), and Eggplant and Walnut Spread (page 9). Substitute orange juice for the Cointreau in the Sweet Potato recipe. Omit the tofu and rice from the Med-Med Soup. Serve the Eggplant and Walnut Spread to the vegetarians while everyone else is eating gefilte fish or at those moments when others are downing chopped liver.

All the recipes in this chapter serve 8–15. Quintuple them for a tiny seder.

KOHLRABI SOUP

Kohlrabi are a cross between cabbage and turnips. Choose smaller kohlrabi with fresh stems. For this or most other kohlrabi dishes, use both the stems and the bulb. We especially like this Romanian soup at Passover (in place of, or in addition to the traditional broth with matzoh balls), because it can be served hot or cold, and because it makes a main dish for vegetarians and vegans.

3–4 kholrabi, peeled and diced

Large head cauliflower, chopped

3 carrots, chopped

1 large onion, diced

$^3/_4$ cup minced fresh dill

$^3/_4$ cup minced fresh parsley

1 tablespoon oil

1 teaspoon basil or thyme

Pepper or red pepper flakes to taste

1$^1/_2$ tablespoons potato starch

2 quarts water, 1 cup reserved

$^3/_4$ cup lemon juice

3 cups canned or fresh tomato sauce

Optional: **1 bunch spinach or kale, chopped**

Garnish: Chopped fresh chives

In soup pot, sauté kohlrabi, cauliflower, carrots, onion, dill, and parsley in oil over medium-high heat for about 7–10 minutes. Add basil or thyme and pepper flakes.

Dissolve potato starch in reserved 1 cup water. Add to pot along with remaining water. Bring to boil, cover, and simmer 30 minutes. Add lemon juice and tomato sauce (and optional chopped greens) and simmer additional 15–20 minutes. Serve hot or chilled. Fresh chives, if you can find them, are the perfect garnish to this soup, and in general are a great match with kohlrabi.   *Serves 10*

MUSHROOM-TOMATO *DUXELLES*

If unadorned turkey seems a bit naked and dry, try this flourless, wine-less, oil-less version of a mushroom duxelles. *Less like a sauce and more like a moist paste, serve it spread thinly on cooked skinless poultry. It also works well with poached or baked fish—but omit the nutmeg.*

2 cups button mushrooms, chopped

1 cup tomatoes, peeled, seeded, and diced

2 cups finely chopped onion

2 large shallots, chopped

2 cloves garlic, chopped

$^1/_4$ cup vegetable stock or defatted chicken stock

Pepper to taste

$^1/_4$ teaspoon nutmeg

2 tablespoons fresh thyme

2 tablespoons fresh parsley

Stir together first eight ingredients in nonstick skillet. Simmer briskly over medium heat until almost all liquid has been absorbed and mushrooms are brown. When almost finished, add thyme and parsley and finish cooking to consistency of loose paste.   *Makes 1$^1/_2$ cups*

GRATED POTATO STUFFING

A simple, tasty, child-friendly stuffing for those allergic to wheat. Useful all year round.

2 large onions, chopped

2 tablespoons oil

10 large potatoes, peeled and coarsely shredded (do not drain released liquid)

$^3/_4$ cup chopped curly parsley

$^1/_2$ cup defatted chicken stock

2 teaspoons salt

In nonstick skillet, sauté onions in oil. In large bowl, combine onions very thoroughly with remaining ingredients. Spoon into turkey. Sufficient for a 12-pound bird.

Vegetable Kugel

For any vegans at your seder, believe it or not, a respectable version of this can be made omitting the egg whites or egg. It will not "set" or slice neatly, but will be spoonable like a stuffing. During the years various of our children have been vegans, we bothered to prepare both versions for the table. (Of course, we wondered why we were investing the energy into catering to people who, after a week without anything resembling even their usual scant protein, were going to be unconscious.)

2 cups matzoh farfel

2 cups water

2 onions, diced

3 stalks celery, diced

3 carrots, peeled and diced

¹/2 cup chopped red or yellow peppers

1 cup grated zucchini

¹/2 cup chopped mushrooms

¹/4 cup chopped parsley

2 potatoes, peeled, grated, and squeezed dry

1 package (10-oz.) frozen chopped spinach, defrosted and drained

Pepper and garlic powder (and salt, if using) to taste

6 egg whites, beaten

1 whole egg, beaten

Soak farfel in water 1 hour. Preheat oven to 375 degrees. Combine soaked farfel thoroughly with remaining ingredients. Pour into greased 9 x 13 x 2-inch pan. Bake 45 minutes.

Serves 10–12

ZUCCHINI AND TOMATO SAUTÉ

2 tablespoons olive oil

6–8 slender zucchini, sliced ¹/₃-inch thick

2 cups cherry tomatoes

Dried basil

In skillet, heat olive oil over medium-high heat, and sauté zucchini and cherry tomatoes until the zucchini are tender but firm. Sprinkle with dried basil and serve.

Serves 8

MATZOH MEAL TOPPED BROCCOLI OR ASPARAGUS

TOPPING:

3 tablespoons Mother's Margarine

2 tablespoons vegetable oil

2 cloves garlic, minced

2 tablespoons Roasted Lemon Juice (page 51) or fresh lemon juice

2 shallots, minced

2 cups matzoh meal

Optional: **¹/₂–1 teaspoon salt. This dish can use it, but omit it if you must.**

VEGETABLES:

4 pounds broccoli florets or asparagus spears, steamed until just tender (may be steamed 1 day in advance and refrigerated)

3 tablespoons Mother's Margarine, melted

1 tablespoon Roasted Lemon Juice or fresh lemon juice

In skillet, heat margarine and oil over medium-high heat; stir in remaining topping ingredients. Sauté until all liquid is absorbed, and matzoh meal is crisp and toasted. (Topping may be made 2 days in advance and refrigerated, or frozen for up to 2 weeks. Bring to room temperature.)

Preheat oven to 325 degrees. Arrange steamed broccoli or asparagus in gratin dish or on oven-proof platter. Spoon over melted margarine and lemon juice. Pat topping across the middle of the dish (this is only possible with, and looks elegant on, the asparagus), or simply sprinkle over vegetables. Bake 15–25 minutes or until hot and topping lightly crisped.

Serves 12

WHOLE WHEAT BANANA KUGEL

While the diabetics and cardiac-concerned must pass this one up, it is a relatively wholesome treat, as whole wheat matzoh retains its bran, wheat germ, and fiber, and bananas are high in potassium. Serve as either a side dish or dessert. Experiment with substitutions for the bananas, such as 2–3 cups diced, steamed winter squash, or add raisins, prunes, diced apples, etc.

6 cups whole wheat matzoh farfel (break up whole wheat matzoh in pieces no larger than $^1/2$ inch, or place in plastic bag and crush with rolling pin or heel of hand)

Cold water

8 eggs

$^1/2$ cup honey

$^1/4$ cup peanut oil

4 bananas, peeled and sliced

$1^1/2$ cups coarsely chopped pecans or walnuts, lightly toasted

Cinnamon

Preheat oven to 350 degrees. Place farfel in bowl and add cold water just to cover. *Immediately* drain farfel so it doesn't become soggy. In separate bowl, beat together eggs, honey, and oil. Stir into farfel.

In greased baking pan or 3-quart casserole, place $^1/2$ of farfel mixture. Cover with banana slices. Sprinkle nuts. Top with remaining farfel mixture. Sprinkle with cinnamon. Bake 45 minutes or just until lightly browned and set.

Serves 12

Bubbe Ida's Gefilte Fish

as interpreted by Grandma Phyllis

The next two recipes do not adhere to the health strictures of this chapter. But if we did not include this one, Bubbe would haunt us for sure.

8 large onions, 6 sliced and 2 chopped

Fish bones*

Varying applications of salt and pepper (Bubbe used "a handful")

3 pounds ground whitefish*

3 pounds ground yellow pike*

5 eggs

1/2 cup water

1/2 cup matzoh meal

3 carrots, peeled and sliced

Red horseradish

*Ask your fishmonger to grind the fish for you, retaining the bones, head, and skin, and wrapping them separately.

To create a fish stock, place 6 sliced onions in stockpot. Wash fish bones thoroughly and place in pot with onions. Add 2 tablespoons salt and 1/2 teaspoon pepper. Add enough water to make the pot half-full. Bring to boil. Turn heat to low and simmer while preparing fish.

In large bowl, combine ground whitefish, ground pike, eggs, and the 2 chopped onions. Add 1/2 cup water. Place 1/3 of fish mixture in bowl of food processor. Process until blended. Transfer mixture to chopping bowl. Repeat with other 2 portions of fish.

When entire mixture is in the chopping bowl, add matzoh meal. Chop until matzoh meal is completely incorporated. Add salt and pepper to taste.

Return fish stock to boil. Form mixture into ovals about the size of the palm of your hand, and drop gently into the boiling fish stock. Turn heat to low; simmer gently 3 hours. After 1 hour, add carrots (and additional water if stock is evaporating too quickly).

Remove from heat and let gefilte fish cool. Remove carrots from stock. Discard stock along with heads, bones, and skin. Refrigerate gefilte fish until ready to serve. Serve with slices of cooked carrot and red horseradish on the side.   *Serves 15*

Marilyn's Passover Brownies

If you're allowed only one unrestricted item, make it one of these Brownies. Enjoy—it's Passover, not Yom Kippur.

6 eggs

3 cups sugar

3 sticks margarine, melted

$^1/_2$ teaspoon salt

9 tablespoons cake meal (a boxed Passover product)

$1^1/_2$ cups cocoa

Preheat oven to 325 degrees. Beat together eggs and sugar until fluffy. Add melted margarine; beat. Sift together salt, cake meal, and cocoa. Add sifted dry ingredients to wet mixture. Combine well and pour into greased 9 x 13 x 2-inch pan. Bake 45–50 minutes.

Makes 20 brownies

Later ...

Having decided not to shoot herself in the head, Dina Katz instead prepared all of the above for her various kosher, vegetarian, diabetic, cardiac-challenged, dieting, allergy-ridden relatives. It took her only twelve days standing in the kitchen and she popped only two varicose veins. Her knuckles were bleeding. But it was all worth it. Her seders were the most spiritual, delicious, and wholesome any of her patients—oops, guests—had ever experienced.

22 The Spill-Etto Festival
Protecting Light Colored Fabrics and Furnishings When Entertaining

A little water clears us of this deed.   —Lady Macbeth

Consuelo read *The Great Gatsby* and never recovered. She *was* Daisy.

When her grandmother passed down the magnificent antique *serape* that had draped her own table, Consuelo thanked her warmly, then tucked it in the attic. Her table would be adorned with cutwork lace, Madeira napkins, and English porcelain—and all of it in white, white, white. The dining room and living room rugs were in palest bisque and eggshell. The sofas were ecru linen. The fainting couch was ivory damask, and the dining room chairs were nubby cream silk. In other words, everything was white.

What spectacular dinner parties she would have! Especially when bedecked in her latest vintage dress composed of virginal Battenburg, eyelet, Chantilly, and Alençon laces with mother-of-pearl buttoned, hand-embroidered pockets.

Consuelo was not deranged, just impressionable. In addition to F. Scott Fitzgerald, her tastes were strongly influenced by the studio-condo of her yoga instructor—the real life human being she most admired, respected, and emulated.

Roshi Tony had snowflake jacquard loveseats, vanilla cashmere floor pillows, and sun-bleached Flokati rugs scattered throughout. White. Until last Wednesday evening when he entertained his favorite students and their families with a fundraiser for the local Intuitive Feng Shui Society.

Consuelo had remained to experience the honor of washing her mentor's dirty dishes. Collecting the white restaurant earthenware, she happened to notice that the used dishes were the only clean objects in the studio-condo.

The loveseats were now French Burgundy, the vanilla cashmere was now chocolate, and the Chicken Vindaloo was playing a vibrant yellow hide-and-seek in the fibers of the Flokatis. Her esteemed master's yoga suit had a giant beet stain on the crotch. She thought of her own decor and her own dress and her own upcoming open house and began to sob huge Daisy tears.

WHAT TO SERVE?

ARTICHOKE CLAM PUFFS

2 packages (10-oz. each) frozen artichokes or 2 cans (16-oz. each) artichoke hearts

1 package (8-oz.) cream cheese or light or fat-free cream cheese

2 tablespoons dry sherry

¹/4 teaspoon Tabasco Sauce

1 can (7-oz.) minced clams, drained

Optional: **Paprika**

Quarter the artichokes. Cook frozen artichokes according to directions (do not overcook). Drain. Place artichokes on broiler-proof plate. Combine cream cheese, sherry, and Tabasco. Mix well. Stir in clams. Spoon mixture onto cut sides of artichokes. Sprinkle with paprika if you want the color. Broil until browned.

Serves 10

ANCHOVY STUFFED MUSHROOMS

24 medium mushrooms

3 tablespoons olive oil

1 can (2-oz.) anchovy fillets

1 garlic clove, finely minced

1 teaspoon fresh lemon juice

$^1/2$ cup fresh soft bread crumbs

$^1/2$ cup minced parsley

Freshly ground black pepper to taste

Olive oil

Preheat oven to 350 degrees. Remove stems from washed mushrooms. Chop stems and sauté in oil for 3 minutes. Chop anchovies and mix with garlic. Add lemon juice, bread crumbs, parsley, sautéed stems, and pepper. Fill caps with mixture. Place in shallow baking dish. Drizzle lightly with olive oil. Bake 15 minutes or until hot.

Makes 24 mushrooms

IRISH SODA BREAD

$3^1/2$ cups sifted flour

$^2/3$ cup sugar

1 tablespoon baking powder

1 teaspoon baking soda

1 teaspoon salt

1 cup raisins

Optional: 2 tablespoons finely chopped pecans

2 eggs, beaten

$1^1/3$ cups buttermilk

2 tablespoons melted butter

Preheat oven to 375 degrees. Sift together flour, sugar, baking powder, soda, and salt. Stir in raisins. Add pecans if desired. In separate bowl, combine beaten eggs, buttermilk, and melted butter. Add egg mixture to dry ingredients and mix lightly. Pour into greased 9 x 5 x 3-inch loaf pan. Bake 1 hour or until done. *Serves 8*

SOUR CREAM COFFEE CAKE

CAKE:

2 sticks butter, softened

1¼ cups sugar

2 eggs

1 cup sour cream

1 teaspoon vanilla

2 cups flour

1 teaspoon baking powder

1 teaspoon salt

TOPPING:

4 tablespoons sugar

1 teaspoon cinnamon

1 cup chopped nuts

Preheat oven to 350 degrees. Cream butter and sugar. Add eggs, sour cream, and vanilla. Sift flour, baking powder, and salt together; stir into egg mixture. Pour half of batter into greased bundt or tube pan.

Combine topping mixture ingredients. Sprinkle half the mixture onto batter in pan. Pour remaining batter on top and then remaining topping. (If you are going to invert the coffee cake, put topping in pan first.) Bake 1 hour.

Serves 10

COLD MARINATED TROUT

3 to 4 large mountain trout

Juice of 6 limes

Juice of 6 lemons

6 bay leaves

Peppercorns

Preheat oven to 150 degrees. Place trout in shallow baking dish. Combine remaining ingredients. Pour over trout. Place in oven for 3–4 hours or until the skin peels, the eyes are white, or until fish flakes with a fork. Serve with dilled mayonnaise and lemon.

Serves 8 for hors d'oeuvres

CHINESE CHICKEN SALAD

SALAD:

1 pound bacon

**5 large fried chicken breasts, cold
(to save time use store-bought fried
chicken)**

1 large head lettuce, shredded

3/4 cup chopped green onions

1 can (3-oz.) chow mein noodles

**1 can (8-oz.) water chestnuts, drained
and sliced**

DRESSING:

**1/3 cup vegetable oil (olive oil may be
substituted for a stronger flavor)**

1/3 cup soy sauce

1 teaspoon dry mustard

2 tablespoons honey

2 tablespoons ketchup

Cut bacon into 1-inch pieces. Fry in pan or microwave on paper towels until crisp. Set aside. Remove bones from chicken and cut breasts into strips. In a large bowl, mix bacon pieces and chicken strips with lettuce, onions, noodles and water chestnuts. Refrigerate until chilled or overnight. Toss with dressing just before serving.

DRESSING: Mix all dressing ingredients in small bowl. May be stored in refrigerator for up to 2 weeks. *Serves 8*

MARINATED CAULIFLOWER

1 large head cauliflower

1 packet Good Seasons Garlic Salad
    Dressing

$1/4$ teaspoon cider vinegar

2 tablespoons water

$2/3$ cup olive oil

$1/2$ cup sour cream

$1/4$ teaspoon chopped scallions

$1/2$ cup crumbled bleu cheese

2 tablespoons slivered almonds

2 tablespoons crumbled bacon

Steam cauliflower 20 minutes. Cool. Mix salad dressing packet with vinegar, water, and oil. Add all other ingredients to dressing. Mix well. Pour over cooled cauliflower. Chill before serving.

Serves 8

FROSTED GRAPES

1 pound seedless grapes

$1/3$ cup honey

2 tablespoons good brandy

2 tablespoons lemon juice

$1^1/3$ cups sour cream

Wash grapes and remove stems. Place in a serving bowl. Mix honey, brandy, and lemon juice. Pour over grapes. Mix well. Refrigerate overnight. When ready to serve, place in dessert dishes and top each portion with $1/3$ cup sour cream.

Serves 4

Cold Lemon Soufflé

$^1/_4$ cup lemon juice

1 teaspoon vanilla

2 envelopes plain gelatin

2 lemons

6 lumps sugar

6 eggs, separated

1$^1/_2$ cups sugar

1 tablespoon cornstarch

2 cups milk, scalded

Pinch of salt

1 tablespoon sugar

1 pint whipping cream, whipped

Cookie crumbs or pralines

Mix lemon juice with vanilla. Pour in gelatin, stir to dissolve, and set aside. Wash lemons. Rub lumps of sugar over them until lumps crumble. This extracts extra oil from the peel. Beat egg yolks with the lumps of sugar plus 1$^1/_2$ cups sugar and cornstarch until mixture turns light and forms a ribbon. Add scalded milk. Cook over low heat, stirring constantly, until custard thickens. Add gelatin mixture. Cool slightly.

Beat egg whites with a pinch of salt and 1 tablespoon sugar until stiff. Fold into custard. Chill, stirring occasionally. When not quite set, fold in whipped cream. Fasten foil collar to extend 3 inches above a 2-quart soufflé dish. Pour in mixture. Refrigerate 4 hours. Sift crumbs or pralines generously over the top surface. Remove collar and serve.   *Serves 8*

TRADITIONAL NOODLE PUDDING (KUGEL) FOR A CROWD

6 eggs

^{1}/2 cup sugar

8 ounces whipped cream cheese

2 teaspoons vanilla

1 stick butter, melted

**1 package (16-oz.) ^{1}/2-inch wide,
flat noodles**

1 pint sour cream

1^1/2 cups cornflake crumbs

^{1}/2 cup brown sugar

1 stick margarine

Blend first five ingredients until smooth. Cook noodles until done. Drain and mix with sour cream. Add egg mixture and stir. Pour noodle mixture into large glass or foil pan. Mix together cornflake crumbs and brown sugar. Cut in margarine until mixture is crumbly. Sprinkle on top of kugel. Freeze unbaked.

Do not defrost before baking. Several hours before serving, preheat oven to 400 degrees. Cover kugel with foil and bake 1 hour. Lower heat to 300 degrees and continue baking for an additional 1^1/2 hours.   *Serves 15–18*

LATER ...

Delicious and clean. A grand success. Except it all looked as boring as a blank sheet of paper. Consuelo, being a young hostess, had yet to learn about garnishes, the decorating concepts of contrasts, warmth, and focal points. Daisy Gatsby, of course, had been trained in all of this since birth. A bouquet of parsley on a bowl of mashed potatoes, tomato or carrot or radish flowers—dangerous though they may be if served as part of the meal—are harmless and gorgeous as decoration. And even though white roses were an obvious and enchanting choice, they weren't the best choice here. The whole place cried out for a big jug of bright tulips or colorful ribbons entwined in the chandelier or ... a magnificent antique *serape* draped on the table.

About the Authors

Laura Szabo-Cohen

Karin Kasdin

Laura Szabo-Cohen is an author, lyricist, and poet acclaimed for her readings, both live and televised. Karin Kasdin is an author, award-winning playwright, and essayist, renowned for her 1997 bestselling book, *Oh Boy Oh boy Oh Boy! Confronting Motherhood, Womanhood & Selfhood in a Household of Boys*, and her plays, "Couples," "Ten Triple A," and "Photo Finish."

Together Laura and Karin authored *Disaster Blasters: A Kid's Guide to Being Home Alone*. They were featured on the TV series "Womanspeak: Women in the Arts." They collaborated (with composer Stephen A. Weiner) on the American stage musical "Spittin' Image." Both indulge their passion for cooking and eating by ... cooking and eating! All in the midst of the hectic, *fin de siècle* life logistics described herein. They live in Bucks County, Pennsylvania. Each has her *own* husband and three children.

Index of Recipe Titles

General Index

General Index

Compelling books from Sibyl Publications

MYTHMAKING: Heal Your Past, Claim Your Future
PATRICIA MONTGOMERY, PH.D.

Empower your future and discover the healing power of myth as you write your life story. Exercises. Thirty myths written by midlife women. "A healing, transformative tool." — **NAPRA ReVIEW** $14.95 ▪ paper ▪ 214 pp

0-9638327-3-5

JOURNEY IN THE MIDDLE OF THE ROAD
MURIEL MURCH

Everywoman's story of taking stock at midlife and discovering the possibilities. "A journey of discovery, of pain, and above all of love." — **The Statesman Journal** "An inspiring memoir. You won't forget this life!" — **MICHAEL ONDAATJE**, author, **The English Patient** $16.95 ▪ paper ▪ 196 pp   0-9638327-4-3

INVENTING OURSELVES AGAIN: Women Face Middle Age
JANIS FISHER CHAN

For the millions of women turning fifty this decade, a conversation among friends about their fears, feelings, discoveries about growing older. "Intimate and engaging, humorous and honest." — **PATRICE WYNNE**, owner, **GAIA Bookstore & Community Center** $14.95 ▪ paper ▪ 202 pp   0-9638327-1-9

REDEFINING SUCCESS: Women's Unique Paths
NANCY JOHNSON

Revealing stories of twenty-four remarkable women and their paths to success. Stunning photos. "The courage and generosity of these women make them modern pioneers and an inspiration." — **MARGIE BOULÉ**, **The Oregonian** $18.95 ▪ paper ▪ 212 pp   0-9638327-5-1

SACRED MYTHS: Stories of World Religions
MARILYN MCFARLANE

PMA Benjamin Franklin Award winner! Thirty-five best-loved stories of world religions for adults and for children 10 and up. Vivid illustrations. "Fosters tolerance and understanding." — **Publishers Weekly** "Priceless treasure, highly recommended." — **Midwest Book Review** $26.95 ▪ hardcover ▪ color ▪ 110 pp   0-9638327-7-8

SPIRITED THREADS: A Fabric Artist's Passion for Life
The Art & Writings of Patricia Roberts Cline
CYNTHIA GRANT TUCKER

PMA Benjamin Franklin Award winner! Her art and journal writings reveal how an artist's passion for her work enabled her to live creatively with a disability. Forty-six B&W photos and twenty-two quilts in full color. "Such love and art are rare—a gift beyond measure." — **MARILOU AWIAKTA**, author, **Selu: Seeking the Corn-Mother's Wisdom** $19.95 ▪ paper ▪ 260 pp   0-9638327-8-6

OH BOY, OH BOY, OH BOY! Confronting Motherhood, Womanhood & Selfhood in a Household of Boys
KARIN KASDIN

Rated Outstanding by Parent Council®! Raising sons to be men who are NOT from Mars is the challenge for mothers of sons. A thoughtful, loving, and hilarious narrative of lessons learned and foibles recounted. "Kasdin tells her boys the truth about life, loves, and body noises." — LENDON H. SMITH, M.D., pediatrician, author, *How to Raise a Healthy Child* $14.95 ▪ paper ▪ 196 pp   0-9638327-9-4

REVISED: THE GODDESS SPEAKS: Myths, Meditations, Symbols & Sacred Sites
DEE POTH

NEW: Now with 31 goddesses and sacred sites around the world where goddesses were revered. Evoke the power of ancient goddesses with this colorful set of 31 meditation cards and book of stories of 31 goddesses. "Uncannily psychic." — *Body Mind Spirit* "Handily accessible guide."— BARBARA G. WALKER
$29.95 book/card set ▪ 31 cards ▪ paper ▪ 190 pp   1-889531-00-6

LOVE, LOSS & HEALING: A Woman's Guide to Transforming Grief
SUSAN TALIA DE LONE, PH.D.

Throught stories, exercises, and meditations, Dr. de Lone unlocks the transformative power of combining East-West traditions and offers concrete, compassionate ways to transcend loss. "Compassionate, wise, and sensitive." — EMMETT MILLER, M.D., author *Deep Healing* "It touches the heart!" — STEPHEN & ONDREA LEVINE, authors *Who Dies?*
$14.95 ▪ paper ▪ 224 pp   1-889531-01-4

SIBYL Publications, Inc.
Tel: (503) 293-8391
Fax: (503) 293-8941
Mail: 1007 SW Westwood Drive
          Portland, OR 97201
Email: sibylpub@imagina.com
Web site: sibylpub.com

Watch for New Cookbook Series in 1999!

1-800-240-8566